KU-034-709

IN SEARCH OF THE FAR EAST

PEOPLE AND PLACES OF THE WORLD

IN SEARCH OF THE FAR EAST

PUBLISHED BY THE READER'S DIGEST ASSOCIATION LIMITED
LONDON NEW YORK MONTREAL SYDNEY CAPE TOWN

Originally published in partwork form,
Des Pays et des Hommes,
by Librairie Larousse, Paris

A Reader's Digest selection

IN SEARCH OF THE FAR EAST

Translated and edited by Toucan Books Limited, London
Translated and adapted by Richard Walker

ISBN 0 276 42050 0

Printed by Printer Industria Gráfica S.A., Barcelona

Contents

COVER PICTURES

Top: *The snow-capped peak of Mount Fuji, Japan's highest mountain, lies within the Fuji-Hakone-Izu National Park some 60 miles south-west of Tokyo.*

Bottom: *A Laotian Buddhist monk. Buddhism is the predominant religion in Laos.*

Old Mingles with New in the Lands of the Far East

The exotic mingling of cultures has always given South-East Asia much of its richness. From the centuries when the missionaries of the world's great religions – Hinduism, Buddhism, Islam and finally Christianity – first reached the region, to modern times when the contrasting gospels of capitalism and communism have each found their fervent adherents, the lands of South-East Asia have shown a remarkable capacity for absorbing outside influences ... as well as for turning them into something uniquely oriental. Holy men, traders and colonists from far-off Europe have all passed through, each leaving their mark for better or worse. But at the same time, the East has always remained the East, faithful to its age-old patterns of life. Great cities such as Tokyo, Bangkok and Kuala Lumpur may buzz to the neon lights and hectic scramble of the late-20th-century consumer lifestyle, but scratch the surface in even the most sophisticated centres and you find a dogged adherence to traditional beliefs and values.

Probably the most striking example of the meeting and blending of old and new, East and West, is Japan. In July 1853, the reclusive island empire was jolted out of over two centuries of strictly enforced isolation from the rest of the world when four US warships under the command of Commodore Matthew Perry sailed into Tokyo Bay with a list of demands from the American President, including a firmly worded request that certain Japanese ports should be opened for foreign commerce. The Japanese found themselves powerless to resist, a humiliating position for a proud people with an ancient military tradition. In order not to follow the example of many of its neighbours by falling under the sway of the Western colonial powers, Japan had to modernise itself. It did so – to large extent by harnessing the military values of loyalty and dedication enshrined in its *samurai* tradition. Just over 50 years later, it was Japan's turn to inflict a humiliating defeat on a Western power – Russia, in the Russo-Japanese War of 1904-5. Later, Japan's astonishing successes at the start of the Second World War were followed by eventual defeat in face of the overwhelming might of the Allies, but again the country bounced back. By the 1990s, a land with less than 3 per cent of the world's population had its second largest economy, rapidly catching up with a worried United States.

Elsewhere in the region, the story is more fluid. Lying at the crossroads of so many trades routes, the various lands of South-East Asia have never been able – as Japan was – to cut themselves off from the outside world. Arabs, Chinese, Portuguese, Dutch, British and French all wanted to trade in the precious spices and other commodities of the Orient. Local empires, meanwhile, rose and fell. From the 8th to 13th centuries, the Buddhist empire of Srivijaya, straddling the Strait of Malacca between modern Indonesia and Malaysia, grew rich from commerce and conquest until it controlled much of Sumatra and western Malaya. Farther east, the Hindu Khmers of modern Cambodia built up an impressive empire with its capital at Angkor, whose ruined temples and sculptures are still among the wonders of the East. From 1350 to 1767 Ayutthaya in Thailand was a capital of outstanding magnificence, trading in teak, sandalwood, sugar, leather, ivory, hides and silks. According to one Dutch visitor, the sunlight reflected so dazzlingly off the gilded roofs of its temples and pagodas that it hurt the eyes from several miles away. None of these realms lasted more than a few centuries, however, and later all – with the exception of Thailand – would fall prey to the trading and colonial ambitions of the European powers. Only in the aftermath of the Second World War would the countries of South-East Asia win back their independence – and in some cases, as in the former French Indochina, only at the price of a bitter military struggle. The Indochinese conflict was later to merge into the nightmare of the Vietnam War, with Americans and local Communists slugging it out in one of the 20th century's most bruising contests between David and Goliath. Neighbouring Cambodia was also to suffer the horrors of the insane and bloodthirsty Khmer Rouge regime of Pol Pot.

And yet through all these centuries of change, certain factors have stayed constant. If the spirit of an 18th-century Japanese returned to his land today, he would of course be baffled by the gleaming high-rise blocks of Tokyo, the congested streets and the high-tech wizardry on display in shop windows. But he would also find much to reassure him that he had indeed come back to the right country. He would find, for example, numerous beautiful gardens, such as Saihoji in Kyoto. He would undoubtedly be puzzled by some of the modern Japanese forms of entertainment – the Western import golf, the sing-alongs of *karaoke* bars. But a bout of *sumo* wrestling would hold no mysteries for him, and in theatres, he would find classic forms of drama, such as *Kabuki* and *Noh,* which would scarcely have changed since his lifetime. In people's homes, he would discover more change, with most city-dwellers (the bulk of the Japanese population) living in tightly crammed apartment blocks, rather than the more spacious wooden homes of old. Even so, most homes would reveal at least one room decorated in traditional style, with reed *tatami* mats on the floor and a small alcove decorated with a favourite painting or calligraphy scroll. In family relationships too, he would notice much that was unchanged: the same deference towards the elderly, of the wife towards the husband, of the daughter-in-law towards her mother-in-law.

Similarly, in South-East Asia, no amount of colonial and 20th-century change has been able to eradicate the old ways of life. Electricity and motor transport, radio and television clearly have made their mark on Malaysian *kampongs* (villages), but again the old family relationships remain, as do the homes perched on stilts and topped with roofs of woven palm leaves. In some remote areas, still older customs survive. In the mountains of northern Thailand live the various Meo, Yao and Karen tribes, easily distinguished among city crowds when they descend for market by their striking black and white or red and blue costumes. They live, as their ancestors have done for generations, by shifting agriculture (that is, by clearing forest and brush, cultivating the land and then abandoning it after two or three years) – though a few less attractive aspects of the modern world have impinged in recent decades, with some tribespeople taking to the illegal cultivation of opium poppies. Indonesia also has numerous such remote groups – from the formerly cannibal Bataks of Sumatra to the Toraja people of Sulawesi.

In religion, South-East Asia presents a complex, interlocking pattern, symbolic of all the cross-currents that have created the region's cultural diversity. Indonesia and Malaysia are officially Islamic, but in both countries the forms of Islam practised by most people are heavily influenced by older Hindu, Buddhist and animist beliefs. Both also have significant Hindu and Buddhist minorities. The Indonesian island of Bali, for example, is almost entirely Hindu, though a form of Hindu that in turn incorporates aspects of Buddhism, beliefs in magic and spirits, and ancestor worship. Balinese religion and everyday life are especially closely intertwined, with sophisticated traditions of art, music, poetry and dancing all forming part of centuries-old religious observances and creating much of the appeal that has made the island Indonesia's favourite tourist destination. To the north, in Thailand, Buddhism is the all-pervasive religion (though this time with a strong dose of Hindu influence). Many young Thai men spend time as Buddhist monks as well as in national service. Communist governments have discouraged the practice of Buddhism in neighbouring Cambodia, Laos and Vietnam, but no sooner have these regimes withdrawn than people have returned to their old beliefs.

As usual, Japan offers a distinctive picture, though once again it is a picture with few clearly defined boundaries. Buddhism and the Japanese folk religion Shinto are dominant, but they are far from mutually exclusive – indeed, a majority of Japanese claim to belong to both. The truth is that while the forms of religion play a noticeable part in Japanese life, few Japanese people are deeply religious – in spite of the growth since the Second World War of new and aggressive sects such as the Buddhist *Sokkagakki* (literally, 'Value Creating Society'). Japanese turn out in force for religious and semi-religious festivals (as well as celebrating a number of Western feasts, such as Christmas and St Valentine's Day), and their shrines and temples are invariably kept in perfect order – but intense religious fervour is rare. To an outsider, it can appear that one of the most important forces binding Japanese society together is the devotion of employees to the company they work for – just as in centuries gone by it was the feudal overlord who drew out the loyalty of his *samurai* followers.

Japan

The land of the 'Rising Sun' has a record that few nations can surpass. Ever since Japan broke out of over two centuries of isolation in 1868, it has regularly surprised the rest of the world, very often by beating it at its own game. Industrialisation was followed by military conquest...which led to eventual defeat in 1945. But the resilience of the Japanese was unbeatable – defeated in war, they went on to build the world's second largest economy. Their land, meanwhile, strung across a long chain of islands, remains one of the most beautiful on Earth, with misty, snow-capped peaks, forests and tumbling mountain streams.

The Land of the Rising Sun

The famous bullet train zipping across ancient paddy fields with snow-capped Mount Fuji towering in the background is the snapshot signature of modern Japan: the 'Land of the Rising Yen', as writer and wit George Mikes called it; a country storming into the 21st century with roots still firmly planted in the 10th.

Since the bullet train first bolted from Tokyo to Osaka in the 1960s, this nation, with no natural resources except their highly distinctive culture, has laid low all of the West's assumptions of technological superiority. Japan is now an economic and industrial world leader. The richest man in the world is Japanese, and six out of the world's top ten banks have their headquarters in Tokyo. Along with the cars, videos and electronic gadgetry, Japanese ideas in architecture, design, food and philosophy have come to touch upon millions of people in the West.

To experts such as Edwin Reischauer, the only American ambassador to Japan to have been born and brought up in the country, the so-called economic miracle is not the most remarkable thing about Japan. What impresses him even more is that the Japanese have achieved economic success while breathing new vigour into their traditional culture.

As much a symbol of Japan as its bullet trains are a pair of rocks, one very big and the other not quite so big, sitting side by side in the sea off southern Honshu. The Japanese took pity on them, strung them together with stout rope, and married them, and every January the vows of the Wedded Rocks of Futamigaura are renewed in a Shinto ceremony that is in equal parts cheerful and solemn. With more than 100,000 other Shinto shrines dotting the landscape, each with its resident *kami* (spirit), the Japanese are bonded to their land like no other people.

Mountain and sea

Like the flexed bow of some giant *samurai* warrior, the islands of Japan arch 1300 miles into the Pacific, from the near-Arctic to the subtropic. When Hokkaido in the north is still locked in ice, the cherry trees of Kyushu are in full bloom.

More than 3000 islands make up the archipelago, though most are mere specks of rock with just enough soil in the cracks to sustain a few scraggy pines. The four major islands account for all but three per cent of the landmass, and nowhere is more than 70 miles from the sea. The Japanese word for landscape is made up of the Chinese characters for 'mountain' and 'water', which perfectly sums up the terrain. Mountain ranges cover three-quarters of the country, and coastlines plunge from dizzy heights into the water, or else leave only pockets of flat land tucked between rugged peaks and the sea. From an aircraft flying along the coasts, the tumbling rivers look like so many white staircases cut into the forested mountainsides. As the abode of the gods and refuge of ancestral spirits, the mountains were sacred until modern times, and even today women may not climb to the summit of the spectacularly beautiful Omine-san range on the Kii Peninsula.

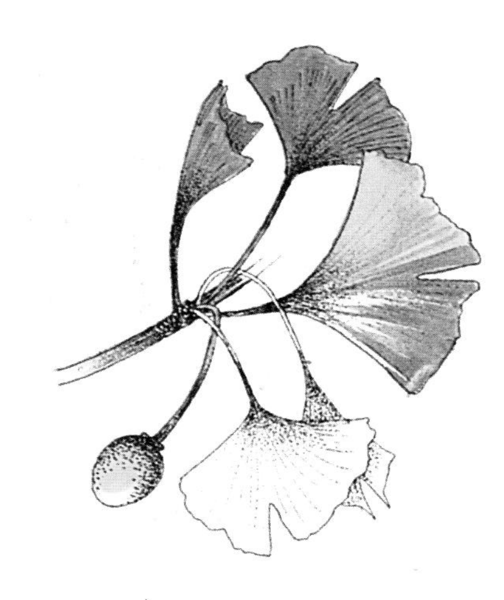

The Ginkgo, *or 'Japanese walnut', so impressed Europeans with its size and beauty that it became one of the symbols of Japan when introduced in the West in the 18th century. The fan-shaped leaves turn golden in autumn, and the tree produces a pulpy fruit that can be eaten raw or grilled like chestnuts.*

The past in Japan merits careful conservation. This thatched rice barn, at Shirakawago in the Japanese Alps, is part of a traditional mountain village created from structures taken from a valley that was flooded to create a dam.

This obaachan *(grandmother) nibbling a rice cake has seen extraordinary changes in her lifetime. The move to the cities and to part-time farming has left only 2 per cent of Japanese working exclusively on the land.*

Previous page: *Matsushima Bay, tucked into the northern tip of the main island of Honshu, is dotted with hundreds of odd-shaped, pine-covered islets that have inspired innumerable paintings and poems. The Japanese reckon it one of the scenic wonders of their land.*

Weather is as much a conversation piece with the Japanese as the British, and with even more reason. Continental and oceanic climate systems play tag around the mountain ranges and cause dramatic local changes. The consequences are particularly dramatic on Honshu, the main island, which is split into contrasting zones by the Japanese Alps that form its backbone. The east coast, called Front Japan, is lapped by the Black Current, a Pacific version of the Atlantic's Gulf Stream, and basks in sunshine throughout the winter, while just across the mountains, Back Japan – the Asia-facing west coast – is being blasted by blizzards and snowstorms of Siberian dimensions. When the east is awash with spring flowers, snow still blankets the western slopes. The contrast is startlingly evident when driving through a mountain tunnel, or in Tokyo station, when a train pulls in, still smothered in snow.

Bizarre natural phenomena are a consequence of such abrupt change. Sendai, in northern Honshu, is noted for its 'snow blossom', a gentle fall of snowflakes that sometimes drift down upon the city from out of a clear blue sky. Likewise, bamboo burdened by a heavy snowfall is a favourite motif of artists and poets.

With so much moisture, all of Japan is luxuriantly green and wooded, and the play of the seasons is a continuous, vibrant symphony. The pink tide of the cherry blossom takes a month to flow north from Kyushu and Hokkaido, and there are nature worshippers who accompany it, island by island, all the way. In autumn, the maples provide the opportunity for a reverse pilgrimage as they blaze their way south in a riot of scarlet.

'When the warmth of spring breathes over the land, the mountains smile, and we are infected with their joy,' says novelist Jiro Osaragi. 'Perhaps people in other lands cannot understand the idea of mountains that smile.' There is near mystical respect for those places where mountain and water mingle most; even

Seaweed cultivation at Kashikojima, on Honshu's Kii Peninsula. The weed is dried, then pressed into sheets. The nori musubi, *a riceball wrapped in a slice of seaweed, is the most popular form of 'Japanese sandwich'. It was invented by a 16th-century warlord who wanted to keep his troops well nourished while on the move.*

Green tea (ocha) *is the national beverage, and plantations are a common sight southwards from Tokyo. Drunk after a meal, it is a perfect complement to the fresh, natural, slightly astringent taste of Japanese food. The best grade is aromatic* gyokuro *(dewdrop), made from the most tender, shaded leaves of the most mature bushes, picked in peak condition.*

Mount Fuji is considered most beautiful in reflection, upside down in one of the five lakes at its base.

This is Jiro Osaragi remembering a sunset on the island-dappled Inland Sea: 'Stately columnar clouds rose; whimsical cloudlets drifted by, and everything was bathed in a constantly mutating illumination of rose and pale green, shades that recall old paintings of the descent of Buddha or of the Western Paradise. Watching that sunset, I could almost hear angelic music falling quietly on the waters. As the moving clouds changed shapes, their edges passed through five different colours. No unified fire, like the sunsets of India or the Philippines, this iridescence blossomed in the elegant semi-tones of the Heian period. If there is a paradise, it will be coloured this way. There will be no primary colours.'

Centuries of co-operative toil in the rice paddies helped to foster the Japanese group mentality, with its instinct for 'doing things together', but technological innovations like the rice transplanter and harvester are making scenes like this obsolete.

Typhoon and volcano

There is a price to pay for all this beauty. Japan is half as large again as Britain, but has more than twice the population – and almost all 123 million are crammed onto the tiny plains, with more than 50 million of them living and working in the Tokyo-to-Kobe industrial corridor along Honshu's Pacific coast. Pollution, though intense, is the least of their problems, for they are sitting on top of a geological time bomb.

The Japanese islands are shards of ocean bed hoisted high by the collision of two of the earth's crustal plates. They trace a particularly hot section of the 'ring of fire' that fringes much of the Pacific with jagged, new-born mountain ranges, and earthquake zones like those of California. Beneath the Sea of Japan, an oceanic plate is burrowing under a plate bearing part of Asia, and frictional heating causes the subterranean rock to melt. There are more than 200 volcanoes in Japan, of which about 60 have erupted since records began; the youngest, Showa Sinzan, burst forth from a Hokkaido potato patch in 1945. In 1990, Mount Unzen of Kyushu erupted after being dormant for about 200 years.

Yet the major threat is from earthquakes. Tokyo's foundations tremble ever so slightly several times a day; the city was wrecked in 1855 and 68 years later, in 1923, which explains the widespread belief that another big quake is overdue. Add to this the ever-present risk of catastrophic damage from the tropical typhoons that can roll in from the Pacific during summer and early autumn, or from a *tsunami* tidal wave that might at any time be triggered by some undersea earthquake.

The people regard these hazards with astonishing equanimity. 'Japanese nature is calm, yet lively and ever-changing,' is the way Jiro Osaragi puts it.

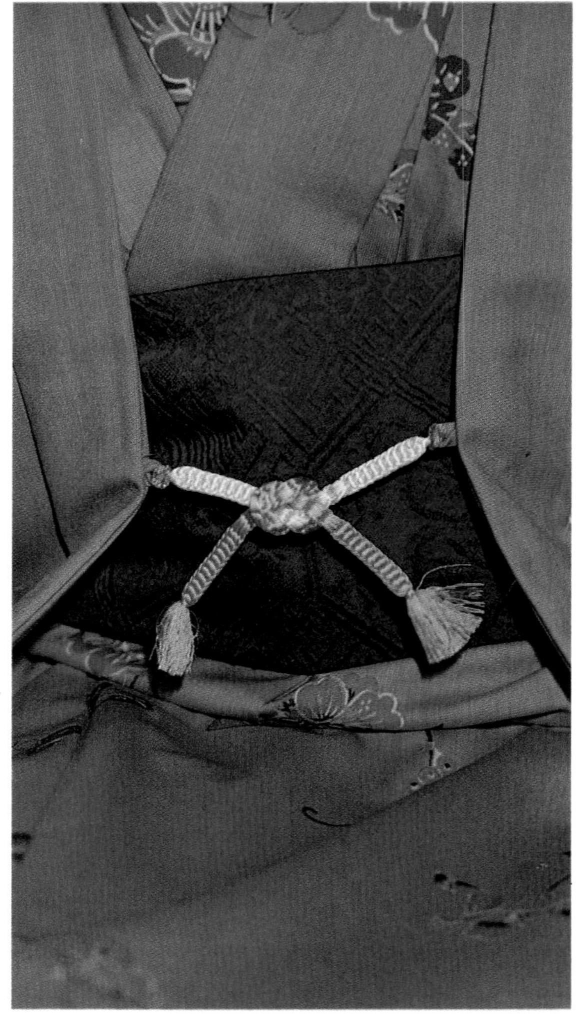

The kimono is the most sumptuous of all national costumes. The basic form goes back to earliest times. Male kimonos are as sombre as women's are decorative – and varied: age, season and social occasion all help to determine the style.

For this reason, kimonos are generally worn only on special occasions, such as weddings, and are often rented, for a new one can cost thousands of yen. As eye-catching as the garment is the obi, *the wide sash that holds the kimono's excess folds.*

A girl dons the obi *at the age of seven. Other accessories include the sock-like* tabi, *and* geta *(clogs) or* zori *(sandals). The only Western accessory tolerated is the wristwatch, though Western-style makeup is an acceptable alternative to the caked mask of tradition.*

Nevertheless, the modern city buildings incorporate the very latest technology in order to minimise damage from earthquakes.

The way of the gods

Like its exquisite lacquer ware, Japan's culture is an accretion of many layers, but at its core it is a simple folk faith placing reliance upon a host of gods to intercede with the forces of nature. This is Shinto, 'the way of the gods' – there are no fewer than 8 million gods or spirits, according to Shinto reckoning.

The *Kojiki* ('Record of Ancient Matters'), which is a sort of Shinto Old Testament, describes the origin of the universe in terms of a giant jellyfish wiggling in the primordial ooze; the Japanese islands are drips from a sacred lance dipped in the stew by Izanagi and Izanami, the Japanese Adam and Eve. The two of them procreated with verve until Izanami expired in much discomfort giving birth to the god of fire. Other offspring included the sun goddess Amaterasu, accredited ancestress to all 123 Japanese emperors up to and including Hirohito, who in 1945 was ordered by his American conquerors to deny the legend.

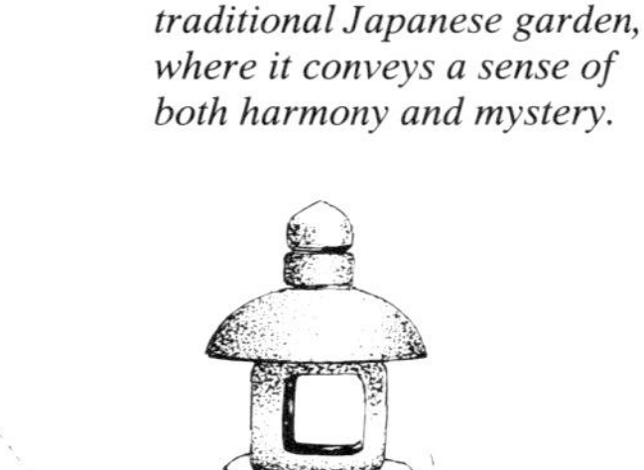

The to *(lantern) is an important element in the traditional Japanese garden, where it conveys a sense of both harmony and mystery.*

The *Kojiki* puts the birth of the Japanese nation at 660 BC. Science is not able to be that precise. Archaeological finds suggest that humans reached the islands more than 30,000 years ago, but much later waves came from the south and from eastern Asia. Among such people, Shinto must have been established. The greatest jump forward, however, came when Buddhism and writing were imported from China. A recognisably Japanese culture first flowered in the Heian period (794-1185 AD), at Nara and then Kyoto. Magnificent temples and pavilions were erected there under the patronage of a sophisticated court aristocracy, so obsessed by matters of elegance and grace that even warriors' armour was held together with gorgeously coloured silk threads. The tea ceremony, flower arranging, Japanese landscape gardening and classic Noh drama all originated at this time.

Court life became so precious that it atrophied, and power passed to a military overlord, or *shogun*, and local barons, *daimyo*, each with his band of retainers – *samurai* – armed with bows and the keenest swords in the world. This is the Japan made familiar to the West through the films of Akira Kurosawa and through James Clavell's best-selling novel *Shogun*. First European contact was not until the 16th century, when the Portuguese pronounced the Japanese 'the best race yet discovered'. This assessment was soon modified. 'They are so crafty that nobody can understand them,' reported the Jesuit leader João Rodriguez.

Misunderstanding is an understatement for what happened next. Japan had second thoughts about tolerating 'barbarians', and about the spread of Christianity, and sealed itself off from the rest of the world for more than two centuries. It became an island of archaic feudalism, a land whose culture was able to develop in a unique state of isolation. A rich merchant class prospered in the great city that rose around the *shogun*'s fortress – Edo, now known as Tokyo – and in Osaka and other cities. So in turn did artists and craftsmen, actors and courtesans. Woodblock prints capture the image and personalities of the *ukiyo* (floating world of pleasure) with stunning effect.

By the mid-19th century the merchants had all the money and the *samurai* elite was impoverished: feudalism had capsized. The United States used gunboat

A corner of the Katsura Imperial Villa, a fragile masterpiece of bamboo and rice paper that was begun in 1630 and took several decades to complete. Set on a river bank amidst exquisite gardens, it is a supreme example of the fusion of architecture with nature, anticipating the best in modern design by more than three centuries.

A Zen monk strides with measured tread from a Kyoto temple. Every element of the garden is in accordance with Zen sensibilities. One of the six major sects of Japanese Buddhism, Zen teaches self-discipline, meditation and self-denial. It provided the philosophical basis of bushido, *the way of the* samurai *warrior, and influenced arts from the tea ceremony to poetry.*

Freshness, simplicity and beauty are the three prerequisites of Japanese cuisine. The critic Roland Barthes described a tray of Japanese food as a work of art in reverse – it arrives as a painting, which, on being disturbed according to the rhythm of eating, becomes a palette. This is the aspect of the traditional Japanese lifestyle that has changed least over the years.

Competence in the basics of the tea ceremony is one of the social graces expected of young women seeking a good marriage – so much so that a descendant of the tea master Rikyu heads a hugely profitable franchise operation certifying teachers and controlling production of utensils using the franchise's name. Such practices may be remote from the teachings of Zen, but the ritual itself has not changed in 400 years. Only the guests partake of the bitter brew. The host concentrates on simmering – never boiling – the water, then scooping it into the tea bowl with a bamboo ladle (above), and whisking it into a froth (right). Every gesture is ritualised. The chawan *(tea bowl) is the centrepiece. Bowls made in Kyoto under the personal direction of Rikyu are to the tea ceremony what Stradivarius violins are to orchestral music. The little ceramic or lacquer caddies that hold the tea powder have also been collected for several centuries (opposite).*

diplomacy forcibly to re-open the country to foreign trade, and the 'barbarians' poured in. Outmoded and at the West's mercy, Japan determined to adapt rather than succumb. Just as it had done with Chinese learning 1200 years earlier, it absorbed Western ideas and technology at breakneck speed. 'Rich land; strong sword' was its motto. *Samurai* sword power was replaced by a Western-style system of parliamentary government; thousands of Western specialists were acquired, particularly from Britain.

Such was the speed of the switch from feudal throwback to modern power that within a generation Japan was able to defeat China and then Russia in wars that stirred further ambition, and finally led to the Pacific carnage of 1941-45.

The living past

Japan has been buffeted by more natural and man-made disasters than most countries, and the wood-and-paper fabric of its traditional culture is desperately fragile, yet the past endures, sometimes in splendour.

Nara has slumbered in retirement ever since the year AD 784, when the capital moved to Kyoto, so it has escaped serious pillage. Set around a large wooded park inhabited by tame deer that enjoy the status of divine messengers, it is a marvellously preserved cradle of *Yamato-damashii*, the Japanese spirit. The nearby temple complex of Horyuji includes the oldest wooden structures in the world.

Kyoto, the imperial capital for 1074 years, is by contrast a thriving city of about 1.5 million people that contrives to retain a great deal of the grace and spirit of another age, even in the face of mass tourism; this is where the entire world comes to see and touch the Japan of legend. Hard by the glass and concrete core of the modern city is the old Gion quarter, which is still the home of the geisha, while aristocratic old ladies in kimonos ford the heavy traffic stream, determinedly impervious to all the many packed and prying *kanto* (tourist) buses.

Kyoto owes its continued existence to one man: American Secretary of War Henry Stimson, who in 1945 called off the bombers that were about to pound it flat; it was consequently the only Japanese city to come through the turmoils of the Second World War almost completely unscathed.

Kyoto is often called the Florence of Japan, and the Florentine scholar and Japan-lover Fosco Maraini agrees, while making an important distinction: 'Florence is Western beauty displayed for all to see; Kyoto is Eastern – its beauty is concealed, a secret to be wrestled from it little by little.' He goes on to explain: 'The idea of a view is entirely Western and entirely un-Japanese. What bad taste, what barbarism, what childishness, to want to see everything all at once. Hence the things that matter in Kyoto are tucked away in little valleys, in green alcoves between the folds of hills: its beauties have to be sought out.'

There is plenty to seek out – 1600 palaces and temples, hundreds of shrines, and all sorts of statistical wonders, from the country's tallest pagoda to its tiniest rock garden. But Kyoto's charm lies as much in its atmosphere as in its objects. It is the city of *shibui* – true Japanese refinement.

Most beloved of all Kyoto's landmarks is the Golden Pavilion (*Kinkakuji*), balanced on the lip of a pond in deep woods to the north-west of the city. It was built in 1397 as a retirement villa for the *shogun* Yoshimitsu. Suspended between water and sky, and radiant in almost any light, it was a shining emblem of Japan's golden age until put to the torch in 1950 by a student monk who found it too beautiful to bear. An exact replica was erected in 1955, but it lacks the age-softened patina of the original.

The fragile beauty and translucent shade of the paper parasol entranced Japan's first Western visitors. Modern Japan has opted for the more substantial, if prosaic, Western umbrella.

Cocoons of white peace

A village of a hundred
houses,
and not one gate
without chrysanthemums

This flower has been the Imperial Japanese emblem for 700 years, and the inspiration for innumerable poems, such as this one by the 18th-century master, Basho.

Each traditional Japanese house is something of a Golden Pavilion, even if on a less ethereal plane. There are no exterior walls, only sliding *shoji* screens, so that the house becomes an element of the garden, resting lightly on the ground by way of raised wooden pillars that leave a gap of a few inches between the floor and the earth. The surrounding patio is open to the sun, or else filters its rays through the translucent rice paper covering of the screens.

Interior rooms are separated by *fusuma*, sliding partitions stretched with heavy paper that provide instant space or intimacy. All furnishing is light and stowable: *futon* bedding that rolls up, collapsible tables, *zabuton* cushions that pack away in cupboards. Decor changes with the cycle of day and night, and when, with a dull thud, the partitions are closed, the ethics and aesthetics of silence come into play, for paper walls can hardly stifle the clink of a tea cup, or even a sigh.

Likou Amata, a turn-of-the-century poet, wrote lyrically of the importance of the paper screen to the Japanese spirit. 'A wooden door is brutal, a wall heavy,' she declared. 'The *shoji* stretched with paper sensitises and refines us ... creates a lucidity between us and life outside, between our soul, the wind and the light ... wraps us in a transparent cocoon, a cell of white peace', which at night becomes a golden shield.

The novelist Junichiro Tanizaki believes that everything Japanese – from the food to people's skins – looks at its best under the 'smoky lustre' of *shoji* light. In his book *In Praise of Shadow*, he describes the effect in a temple: 'The light from the pale white paper, powerless to dispel the heavy darkness of the alcove, is instead repelled by the darkness, creating a confusion where dark and light are indistinguishable. Have you not sensed a difference in the light that suffuses such a room: a rare tranquillity not found in ordinary light?'

Such philosophical thoughts aside, traditional Japanese architecture is a brilliant demonstration of functional simplicity, based upon modular construction techniques that are now commonly adopted in international design. The basic unit is the *tatami* mat; this floor covering of braided rice straw is made in standard three feet by six feet sections. Calculating by numbers of *tatami*, a grid floor plan is drawn up – there could be a three-*tatami* room, a six-*tatami* room, and so on. From this the placement of walls, roof and garden is determined, all measured in terms of *tatami* units. The carpenter and *shoji* and *fusuma* makers also work to this scale, so that once the size of the house is determined, construction proceeds smoothly. (*continued on p.25*)

A Shinto priestess, or miko, *on duty at a garden shrine wears the traditional white and red robes of her office. A priestess's duties include guiding worshippers and visitors round the shrine as well as taking part in religious ceremonies. She must be unmarried, but may also have a part-time job – as a teacher perhaps or as a nurse.*

Sunrise over a sacred enclosure of trees captures the essence of the Japanese sense of sanctity. The feeling is most intense at the shrine of Ise, the forest-guarded shrine of Amaterasu Omikami, the sun goddess, and so sacred that only the imperial family may enter.

Bonsai *(tray planting) is an extreme expression of the Japanese obsession with trees. Though the roots of the craft go back 600 years, the term dates from as recently as the 19th century, and a number of the techniques involved in growing and training forests only a foot high were not developed until early in the 20th century.*

The Japanese garden has been described as nature captured and intensified. With its controlled harmony, seasonal splashes of colour and tinkling waterways, it is a metaphor for Japan itself. Each plant carries its own message, of longevity, happiness or beatitude.

Samurai *once gathered strength from contemplating this rock grouping at Kyoto's Nanzenji temple. The stones are an evocation of immortality, doubtless soothing to warriors. For more than 300 years, Zen monks have been raking the sand into spirals of infinity.*

The martial arts

Kendo – the way of the sword – dates back to the 12th century. With its 'sudden death' climax, its legends and its masters passing on their secrets only to those deemed of worthy character, it is the quintessential form of *budo*, as the martial arts are collectively known. Much of the modern equipment – the bamboo stave, faceguard and breastplate – was introduced comparatively recently in the last century, when the *samurai* class was dissolved and real-life swordplay discouraged. The object, however, remains the same: to strike the opponent's head, torso and wrist, and then to finish him off with a ritualised thrust to the throat.

Speed, co-ordination and the application of power at just the right instant are the same qualities demanded by the several forms of *budo* that are now practised throughout the world. The most famous of them, judo, is another 19th-century adaptation of an ancient fighting technique, and it is just as rigorously codified. Yet another, *Aikido,* relies even more than judo upon the knack of turning against an opponent the thrust of his own attack; it has a number of its own throwing techniques and 'pain holds'.

Karatedo, meanwhile, is unarmed combat turned into a kind of flying ballet, as swift and graceful as it is potentially lethal. Developed in the Ryukyan islands of the far south, the karate techniques were a closely guarded secret until the 1920s, when they were introduced throughout Japan. Hands, arms, legs and feet are used to block and strike at vital parts of the opponent's body.

Many top business executives practise *kendo* for its mix of mental and physical exercise, as well as for its social cachet. Others find release in archery, conducted in the garb of the *samurai* era, and directed towards achieving a truly serene command of mind over muscle. Perfection becomes sublime when the master bowman no longer feels the desire ever to release his arrow.

The entire process had been standardised by the 17th century, with the canons of Zen reinforcing a natural preference for clean and simple lines. Westerners may regret that a diminishing number of Japanese still live in this traditional style of house. The majority of Japanese, however, have happily accepted the change to a Western style.

Ancient Chinese records indicate that women ruled parts of early Japan as priestess-chieftains, and it was not until feudal times that women became completely subordinate to men. Certain high positions in the Shinto priesthood are reserved for women, like this naishoten serving on the ceremonies council of the Imperial household.

Tea in the garden

The Zen-fired quest for exquisite simplicity achieved its ultimate expression in the act of taking tea in a little garden hut. Tea was first brought to Japan from China by Zen priests who recommended it as an aid to meditation. The upshot was *chanoyu*, the tea ceremony. As the culmination of a ritual meal served in tiny portions, every action and artefact connected with the ceremony has been refined to the limit of human ingenuity. Enormous attention is given to the utensils, and ancient tea bowls and caddies can command correspondingly enormous prices. Slight imperfections add to their value, for as the saying of the tea masters goes: 'The full moon is not pleasing in a cloudless sky.'

Guests enter the garden singly, crouching through a low doorway and rinsing mouth and hands at a stone basin before stepping on a path (*roji*) which symbolises the first stage of meditation. The teahouse itself is small and constructed of natural materials whose weathering accords with the Buddhist concept of the impermanence of all things; a flower and scroll painting appropriate to the season or occasion are placed in the *tokonoma* alcove as sole decoration.

Guests drink the frothy, bitter, green tea called *maccha* in turn, sharing bowls that are carefully washed each time by the host, whose every gesture is a balance of studied serenity. Like Zen itself, *chado* – the way of tea – cannot be acquired from books, but is passed down from master to disciple. There are three schools, each headed by masters claiming descent from Sen no Rikyu, tea master to the 16th-century warlord Hideyoshi.

It is related how Hideyoshi once arranged to take tea at a time when Rikyu's celebrated morning glories

A Shinto priest performs a ceremony of ritual purification. The dangling strips of paper represent prayers. Participants are expected to have cleansed their bodies inside as well as out, by abstaining from alcohol, tea, onions and other strong-flavoured foodstuffs, and also from any food of foreign origin.

Framed by the gateway of a Shinto shrine, a priest assumes the spirit of the resident kami (deity). His task is to assure harmonious relations between the human and the spirit world. He does not offer moral guidance, and he does not preach, since human speech is considered impure.

would be in full bloom. The warlord arrived to find the master's garden stripped bare, and a solitary morning glory displayed in his *tokonoma*. Rikyu explained that he had picked that bloom as the essence of his garden, and had destroyed all the others lest they detract from it.

If Hideyoshi and Rikyu represent two extremes of the Japanese character, it is sobering to learn that Rikyu eventually irritated Hideyoshi to such an extent that he was ordered to commit *seppuku*, ritual suicide.

A tea garden is intended to concentrate but not distract the mind; its subdued hues, stepping stones and mossy stone lanterns, tinkling bamboo water spout and rough-lashed fencework, make it particularly pleasing to Western eyes. Garden art began as a Chinese import, but was very soon transformed by the nature-venerating sensibilities of the early Japanese. It was codified seven centuries ago according to the *yin* and *yang* contrast principles – feminity and virility, shadow and light, object and space. The full-blown classic Japanese garden of knolls and hillocks artfully planted with pine, maple and cherry, carp-filled ponds and a stream crossed by little bridges and stepping stones, is a self-contained world. A supreme example is in the gardens of the Katsura villa in Kyoto; they took 40 years to create out of what had been paddy fields, and have been carefully tended for 300 years.

The pursuit of Zen ideals produced extremes of expression, exemplified in two other world-famous Kyoto gardens. Saihoji is better known as the Moss Temple for the 50 varieties of moss that thickly carpet every nook of its garden, created more than 600 years ago. Ryoanji is as arid as Saihoji is lush: it consists of 15 rocks arranged in groups of seven, five and three, set in gravel that monks of the Rinzai sect have been raking into rills for about as long as the moss has blanketed Saihoji. The monks meditate as they rake.

The crowing cocks on this portable shrine recall how the sun goddess Amaterasu Omikami had to be enticed from a cave in which she had hidden herself, plunging Japan into darkness. One of Japan's favourite legends, the re-emergence of Amaterasu Omikami is cause for hearty celebration.

The Gion Festival in Kyoto commemorates an epidemic in the year 869. The response to the emperor's appeal to the gods for help was so swift and positive that thanks have been offered ever since. A procession of huge floats trundles to the Yasaka Jinja shrine, where the gods of prosperity and good health preside.

Entwined faiths

Saturated by religions – so that a majority owe at least nominal allegiance to two at the same time – the Japanese are casual in their observances, unfettered by dogma. Rather, they mix and match ritual and ceremony according to a calendar of social convention.

When a Japanese is born, the baby is brought to the local Shinto shrine to be presented to its *kami* (spirit), and Shinto ceremony marks the child's passage past the ages of three, five and seven. Shinto also has a monopoly on weddings, but the Japanese die as Buddhists, with a temple priest officiating.

Shinto goes to the Japanese soul; it is the indigenous belief practised for more than 2000 years. Shrines dedicated to its numberless *kami* are everywhere; the most sacred, that of the sun goddess, stands at Ise, east of the first capital facing the rising sun across the Pacific. Innumerable lesser shrines, each with its *torii* gateway, mark the spirit domain of ancestors, real and mythological, rice deities, emperors, military heroes, or simply striking works of nature: a big mountain, a pretty waterfall, a venerable tree or an odd-shaped rock.

Hand clapping gains the *kami's* attention, and help may be sought in passing a school exam, or combating sickness, but Shinto has no doctrine, no texts, no theology, not even a concept of right and wrong. There is no Japanese word for 'sin'; the nearest, *tsumi*, refers to ritual impurity, the main Shinto concern.

This boy, aged eight or nine, will serve as a sacred page at the Yusaka shrine through the two days of the Gion Festival. For all the delight in religious festivals, the gods do not weigh heavily on Japanese minds – especially those of the young. In recent polls, less than 20 per cent of Japanese youth laid claim to any religious belief.

To cope with life's profounder questions, there is Buddhism, which teaches 'enlightenment', with the prospect of eventual heavenly liberation from repeated, painful cycles of life and death. There are many Buddhist sects, all stressing the temporary nature of the material universe. While Shinto taught the Japanese to cherish cherry blossom, Buddhism taught them to value its impermanence – the scattering of its petals is the moment of truth, as well as of perfect, fleeting beauty.

A constant celebration

Festivals have been called the gateway to Japanese culture, and most have a Shinto basis. These are the *matsuri* – bewildering in their number and form. There are *matsuri* dedicated to animals and fish, vegetables and flowers, to historic happenings and every stage of the rice cycle. Their purpose is to give thanks to the *kami*, and once this has been attended to, there are processions and entertainment.

A characteristic feature of many *matsuri* is the portable shrine, called a *mikoshi*, in which the *kami*, usually represented by some sacred emblem, is carried around the area under his or her protection, often by gangs of youths stripped to loincloths. Sake – rice wine – is the drink of the gods, and it does wonders for participating mortals as well. One of the more revealing sights Japan has to offer is that of snoozing drunks lying on a carpet of cherry blossom and broken bottles after a particularly enthusiastic spring festival.

Summer festivals are the most spectacular. They usually take place at night and were originally intended to ward off the diseases that accompanied the long rainy season. Participants wind around the streets or the paddy fields, brandishing pine torches and calling on the *kami* for protection. One of the most celebrated of these *natsu matsuri* is that of Gion, which dates back to the 9th century when Kyoto withstood a virulent plague. Two days of celebrations reach a climax when about 30 richly-decorated giant floats, weighing as much as 12 tons, are dragged to the Yasaka Jinja shrine.

Death and the dead are the business of Buddhism, so the great festival of O-bon is a Buddhist rite, and an occasion for a mass exodus to ancestral villages. The spirits of the dead are escorted by lanterns from the cemeteries to their former homes, and for days the living and departed hold a party together. Then, under a full moon, the dead are escorted back to their graves.

Sacred and secular mix easily where the gap between the human and divine is so slight, and Japan's immortal guardians are not the kind to stand in the way of progress. Now that the transistor and silicon chip have supplanted rice as the sustainer of life, the gods have a new order of priorities. Okuninushi no Mikoto, host god at Izumo, has lately had his duties extended to include the management of company mergers. Inari, a popular rice god, is traditionally supposed to ensure a good harvest. Today, in Tokyo, Inari has more pressing commitments as the guarantor of profit for the businessmen who maintain his shrines with their statues of little grinning foxes, Inari's mysterious messengers.

Even big-city traffic has to halt when the shrine bearers weave their noisy, jolting way down a street, with frequent pauses for sake. The spirits appreciate a rollicking ride.

The Land of Modern Miracles

At 2am on the hot, dank morning of August 10, 1945, Emperor Hirohito addressed the Supreme War Council in a deep bomb shelter beneath the Imperial Palace gardens in Tokyo. Before each stiff-necked warlord lay a copy of the Allied call for immediate and unconditional surrender.

The homeland was encircled, and their incinerated cities glowed like so many *hibachi* grills from constant American bombing. Hiroshima had been vaporised on August 6, and a second atomic bomb had just been dropped on Nagasaki three days later. The Council was deadlocked between those who reasoned that resistance was useless, and the militarists, steeped in the death-before-dishonour code of the *samurai* warrior, who wanted to carry on the fight, whatever the cost.

The Son of Heaven spoke slowly, a tremor raising the pitch of his voice as he advised: 'Endure theunendurable.' He said it again in a broadcast. All of Japan listened, incredulous, transfixed by the strange voice speaking in archaic classical Japanese. Hirohito had never before spoken in public, let alone on the radio. 'The war situation has developed not necessarily to Japan's advantage,' he told his people, in one of the great understatements of history. 'The enemy has begun

Traders do brisk business along the approach to a Shinto shrine in Tokyo. Before buying your incense, it is proper to put a small coin in the monk's begging bowl.

to employ a new and most cruel bomb ... should we continue to fight it would not only result in the ultimate collapse and obliteration of the Japanese nation, but also it would lead to total extinction of human civilisation ...'

The emperor's word was Japan's bond. On September 2, a surrender was signed on board the US battleship *Missouri* in Tokyo Bay. General Douglas MacArthur, the Allied commander, took charge. His orders were to transform a martial, tradition-bound Oriental society into a docile Western-style democracy, and he had to rely largely upon the Japanese themselves to do it, if only because very few Americans could speak the language, let alone fathom the culture.

The Japanese dutifully – even enthusiastically – obeyed this lanky *gaijin* (foreign) *shogun.* Within a month of the surrender, MacArthur issued a directive giving women the vote and abolishing all laws restricting personal freedom. Within a year, he had imposed a constitution that enshrined these changes; it also contained the crucial Article 9 which renounced Japan's right to 'wage war'. The Japanese education system was substantially reshaped to lay more stress on American ideas of individualism, and a tentative start was made on dismantling the *Zaibatsu*, the all-powerful

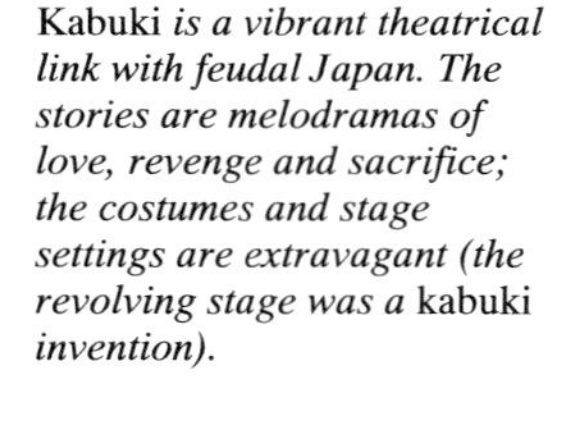

Kabuki *is a vibrant theatrical link with feudal Japan. The stories are melodramas of love, revenge and sacrifice; the costumes and stage settings are extravagant (the revolving stage was a* kabuki *invention).*

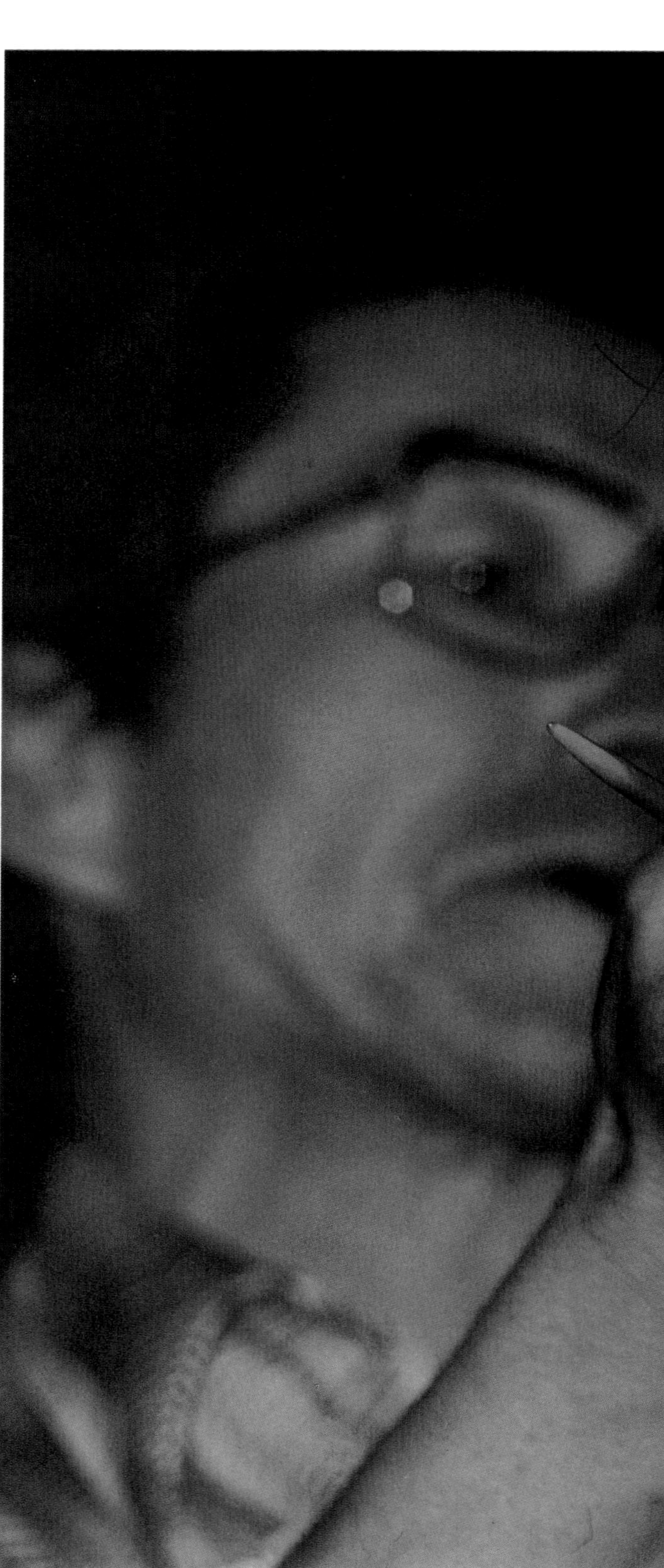

business cartels that had powered Japan's war machine. Hirohito was 'humanised'. On January 1, 1946, he disclaimed his divinity in a radio broadcast to the nation, and then he published a poem:

The pine is brave
that changes not its colour
with the weight of the snow.

The snow cleared, and the pine did not change its colour, but only grew stronger and stronger. Imperialism had failed them, so instead the pragmatic Japanese changed direction with all the energy and unity of purpose that had marked their leap from feudalism less than a century earlier: now they would change from military expansion to seemingly unstoppable economic and industrial success.

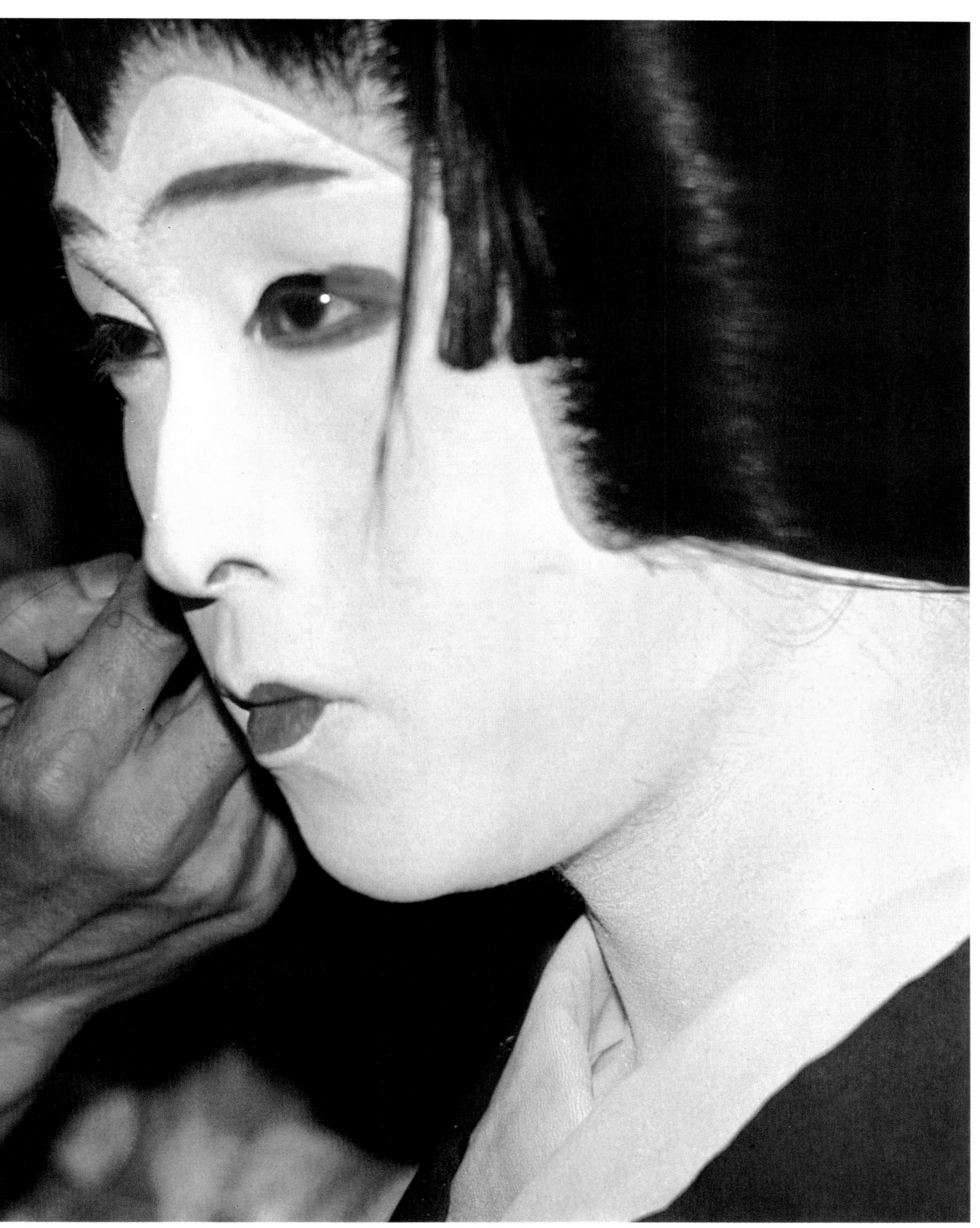

All the performers – including this ravishing 'actress' – have been male since women were banned in the 17th century for being too lewd.

Is he good? Is he evil? Once completed, this kabuki *actor's* kumadori, *or heavy make-up, will leave no one in any doubt. An accompaniment of ear-piercing flutes, drums and the gentle three-string* shamisen *frays or soothes the nerves, as required by the action.*

Tokyo – city of magnificent madness

Tokyo is staggering – a seething cauldron of all that Japan has achieved, and lost, in the performance of its post-war miracle.

A thousand-bomber raid in March 1945 created a firestorm that left only charred rubble as far as the eye could see. Out of the rubble has arisen the most challenging, and exhausting, metropolis on earth. It is also the most impermanent; putting up buildings, tearing them down, and then rebuilding – all of this proceeds at such a pace that even Tokyoites sometimes get lost.

Close to 12 million people live within 20 miles of the Imperial Palace, most of them imbued with the kind of work ethic and group consciousness that make other nations look sluggish. Half a day is barely sufficient to

The prologue is over, the music has stopped, and the characters sit absolutely still, building tension for what is about to happen ... Noh *is theatre stripped to the bone – austere, solemn, with only symbolic props. Hardly changed in 600 years, it is performed to a droning chant, reminiscent of classical Greek drama.*

Noh *is the very opposite of* kabuki: *it is aristocratic, and so slow moving that it becomes mesmerising. The central figure in a* Noh *play is a masked and sumptuously robed protagonist known as the* shite, *who might be a warrior, a noble lady or even a supernatural being.*

The masks are superb pieces of sculpture. With a subtle head movement, the smile of the young girl becomes charged with melancholy.

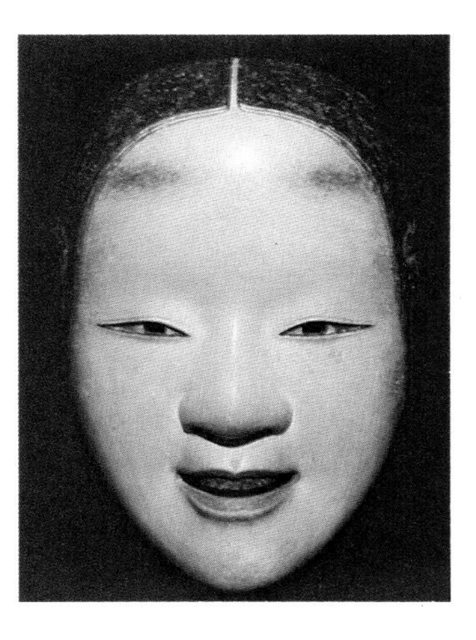

The mask stylises performance and muffles and hollows the voice. Everything is stylised in Noh. *Thus, an old man is always wrinkled, bald and bearded.*

drive the dozen miles to the port of Yokohama, such is the density of traffic. Walking, or rather shuffling, is even worse: this is the city of the pedestrian bottleneck. Pollution in the 1960s reached choking point. Mount Fuji vanished behind a veil of smog, and soot encrusted the cherry trees that ring the Palace gardens. The enforcement of rigid smoke and exhaust emission standards rescued the city from respiratory failure. Beloved Fuji-san can be contemplated once more, and the cherry trees only need a regular wipe-down. The distressed can catch their breath with a squirt of coin-in-the-slot oxygen, Japan's latest contribution to urban living, along with the robot restaurant greeter.

Tokyo is the reverse of Mount Fuji, which when you reach it turns out to be bleak and barren. Gross and ugly at first sight, Tokyo's concrete canyons reverberate with an irrepressible vitality, and chaos resolves itself into richly creative variety. 'The kind of energy you find in Tokyo could flower only in an atmosphere where there are virtually no rules to break,' reasons Jared Lubarsky, a resident writer. So the architect can go as crazy as the neon sign designer – because however grotesque his latest extravaganza, it will soon be superseded by the next one.

The anarchy is kept in check by collective self-discipline, for age-old Japanese values are hardly expunged by the extraordinary change in fortune that has made this the world's wealthiest society. This is the city that can buy anything, and appears to be in the process of doing so: recent acquisitions range from Van Gogh's *Sunflowers* to a famous Coney Island merry-go-round; and Tokyo's Disneyland, identical to (but costlier than) the originals in California and Florida, has been drawing 10 million Japanese fans of Mickey-san every year since 1983.

Sunset along the Ginza – just before the lights blaze on – reveals the murky underside of the Japanese economic miracle. Gauze masks are frequently worn to cope with colds and throat infections, problems aggravated by over-crowding. Carbon dioxide and noise levels are monitored and displayed at major intersections.

The hub of affluence is the Ginza, the fabulous eighth of a square mile where elite stores jostle for space with around 150 restaurants, perhaps 1700 bars, and at least 330 art galleries. Yet Tokyo has no centre; it is a welding job, patching together 23 wards and more than 40 cities, towns and villages, each with its own history and distinctive personality. Akasaka and Asakusa may sound confusingly alike, but one is a sophisticated melee of embassies and tycoon-tending geisha retreats, while the other is the last stronghold of the true *Edokko,* the Tokyo Cockney, still with huddled streets of traditional wooden houses; both are worlds apart from Harajuku, the boutique haven where fashionable youth preens itself.

Like some science-fiction monster, Tokyo gobbles up whole slabs of alien culture and regurgitates them in its own image. Take *Kurisumasu* – that's Christmas, in Japanese. Tokyo celebrates the great Western *matsuri* with a massive spending spree, and that jolly *kami* Santa Claus can be seen everywhere. But jingle bells and tinsel are merely a prelude to *O-Shogatsu.* This is when homes are decked with pine, bamboo and plum blossom, and temple bells throughout the country ring out 108 times to cast down each of the 108 evils that afflict humanity, and shrines are crowded with worshippers and glow with the light of innumerable lanterns. *O-Shogatsu* is an ancient and distinctly Japanese celebration of New Year.

Japan is a man's world, except in the home, where the wife rules – unless dominated by the mother-in-law, a formidable figure in many traditional families.

To savour Tokyo at its most frenzied, a visitor needs to brave Shinjuku Station during the morning rush hour, when trains are jammed to three times their capacity with the help of strong-armed 'pushers'. Nine rail and underground routes converge on Shinjuku, disgorging 2 million passengers every day; the station includes a vast underground shopping complex, and it has 60 exits. Depending upon the exit taken, the rider surfaces in a 21st-century landscape of shopping plazas and supposedly earthquake-proof skyscrapers ... or in a sleezy pornocopia of bars, strip joints and sex enterprises of every description, including a lively selection of 'love hotels': fancifully-designed places that glow pink at night.

Living in miniature

There are at least 10,000 love hotels in Japan. In fact, up to half of the couples checking into a typical establishment are married – to each other – and what they are seeking is simply the privacy so frequently denied them in their tiny crowded homes.

A quarter of Tokyo's residential accommodation averages less than 30 square yards, and most flats in the city's many concrete blocks are hardly larger than a fair-sized Western room. Land prices in central Tokyo are the highest on earth, and as a result space is the most precious commodity of all; the Japanese have even been prepared to sacrifice chunks of their beloved mountains to use as landfill in order to wrest living space from the sea.

The national genius for miniaturising everything from trees to poetry has found its latest, and most practical, expression in capsule living. The Nakagin building in the heart of Tokyo looks like a Brussels sprout, with a central stem bearing clusters of portholed cubes, each one a mini-sized, self-contained bedsitter. A capsule hotel in Sinjuku has several restaurants and swimming pools, and an American-style wedding chapel perched on the roof. The accommodation consists of about 700 bed-sized moulded plastic cocoons into which guests crawl; each is equipped with TV and telephone.

Living in the Nakagin may be cramped, but each unit has what hundreds of thousands of Tokyo homes still

Flower arranging (ikebana) – in Japan has no more to do with sticking plants in a pot than the tea ceremony has to do with the quick cuppa. Only a few blooms and sprigs are used in any one piece – the art is in their selection and placement. Like the tea ceremony, ikebana is now part of the standardised training for young Japanese women and, like landscape gardening, it is one of the Japanese arts to have had a big impact on the West.

lack – a bath. Fortunately, the Japanese believe in sharing their pleasures, and communal bathing comes near the top of their list. Shinto concepts of ritual purification, and Japan's abundance of natural hot springs, help to explain how the social soak gained such a hold in the country.

Washing is not strictly what this is about – people are required to scrub and rinse themselves squeaky-clean before entering the scalding hot bath where, submerged to the chin and divested of the trappings of social rank, they exchange gossip with an informality that is rarely, if ever, possible elsewhere. This is pure bliss, Japanese-style. It is even possible to enjoy a hot bath while suspended high above the spectacular coastline of the Kii Peninsula south of Osaka, in a device known as the cable car bath.

The Japanese contradiction

After 400 years of defying Western analysis, the Japanese are popularly perceived as a bundle of contradictions: cruel and gentle, arrogant and humble, selfish and polite, materialistic and ascetic, exclusive and welcoming, westernised and inscrutably oriental. During the Second World War, the American anthropologist Ruth Benedict was commissioned to delve into the psyche of the enemy. The book she wrote as a result of her researches became a classic, and its title summarised her verdict on the Japanese character. She called it *The Chrysanthemum and the Sword.*

The Japanese see such contradictions as only natural. Just like life and death, 'holiness and profanity, splendour and gloom form the dual basis of man's culture', argues Kyoto University Professor Mitsukuni Yoshida. But few people act out the phenomenon so visibly. Even the name Japan is equipped with a split personality. In Japanese, it can be either Nippon or Nihon. Nippon is tough, assertive, masculine; Nihon is more feminine, gentle, giving. Usage depends upon circumstances.

A crucial ingredient in the glue that holds Japanese society together lies in the teachings of Confucius, which reached Japan about the same time as Buddhism. Confucianism is defunct as a religion, but its concept of *rei* – roughly translated as good manners – and loyalty to authority profoundly influence behaviour. The bow, with its infinitely subtle variations and gradations, is a good example of this. So is Tokyo's remarkably low crime rate.

Japan's matching of East and West is in evidence in this wedding group. Most brides prefer to marry in traditional dress, topped by the elaborate bunkin-takashimada *headdress, and few Japanese feel truly wed without the nine sips of sake prescribed by Shinto ritual. In better-off families, the bride changes her dress several times during the wedding banquet. The going-away dress will be Western, and so will the honeymoon: Hawaii and Australia are favourite destinations. There is great social pressure on women to be married by 25, and men by 28 – at the latest. Families are small (the statistical average is 1.7 children) and so is the divorce rate, which is just as well when one considers the cost of weddings: over £20,000 is considered normal.*

The family is the basis of Japanese life, and family spells authority. The entire nation operates as one big family, as do its big business corporations, and so on down to the domestic unit, which in some ways recalls the European family before the industrial revolution. In rural homes, everyone still sits according to their place in the hierarchy. The centre spot is reserved for the father, and opposite him sits the son's wife, who is lowest in the pecking order. Family members refer to one another by their position rather than name. There is big brother *(ototosan)*, big sister *(onesan)*, little sister *(imotosan)*, and so on, with the male line of succession taking precedence.

The emphasis on individualism so often seen in the West is regarded as selfish and extremely inconsiderate. As the favourite Japanese expression puts it, 'the nail that sticks up gets hammered down'. The individual Japanese exists as a 'me' merged into the 'we' of family and community. This attitude is instilled from infancy: Japanese toddlers are outrageously spoiled, while being gently bonded into a system of dependence and obligation. The Christian concept of sin, with reward or punishment in an afterlife, is alien to Japanese thinking. Obligation takes its place, as is quickly apparent in any conversation. A Japanese equivalent of 'thank you' is *sumimasen*, which translates as 'you will excuse me but I am greatly indebted to you'.

'For Japanese, the supreme source of guilt is not violating an immutable set of moral principles such as the Ten Commandments, but the sense that they have hurt someone else by failing to behave as that person expected,' states Robert Christopher in his book *The Japanese Mind*. Here is the key to Japanese politeness, which, rather than speaking the truth, defers to the truth of others.

In his novel, *The Lake*, Yasunari Kawabata captures the attitude in an exchange between a teacher and a pupil who stays silent when the rest of the class chuckles over a passage he has just read out.

> 'You do not laugh, Miss Onda?'
> The young lady remained silent.
> 'Miss Onda, you do not find this amusing?'
> 'No sir.'
> 'All the same, you should have laughed like the others.'

And yet, a Japanese commonly contrives to combine commitment to the group with driving personal ambition. 'He is not a weak-willed yes-man,' stresses Edwin Reischauer in *The Japanese Today*. 'In contrast to normal Western perceptions, social conformity is no sign of weakness but rather the proud, tempered product of inner strength.' When this snaps, the results can frequently be violent, as in the case of the explosive

Two 7-year-olds present themselves at their local shrine to seek the kami*'s protection through the coming years. The* shichigosan *ceremony in November is a gala occasion.*

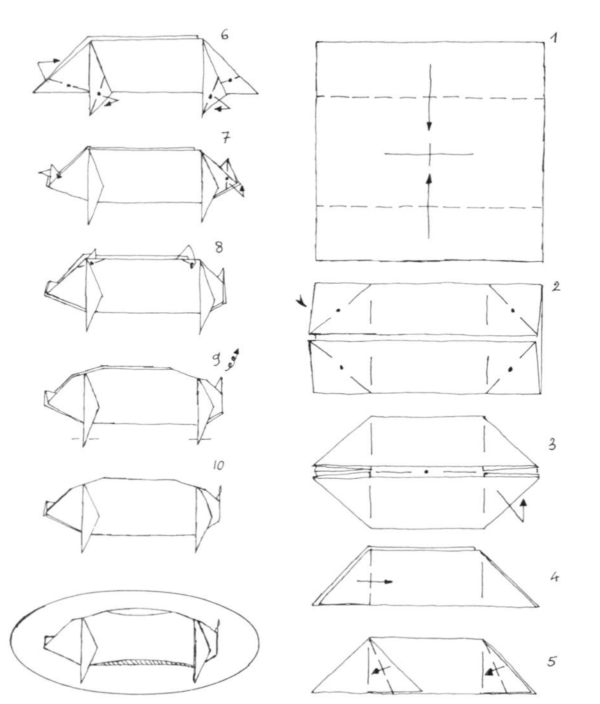

Origami, the art of folding paper, is a Japanese children's hobby that has been taken up world-wide. Instructions for making this little paper pig are printed the Japanese way, right to left. Enthusiasts vie in the creation of new and ever more complex designs, and there is even an International Origami Research Centre with headquarters in Tokyo. Just as paper kites were first flown as symbolic offerings to the gods, origami has religious origins. It is linked to the folded paper strung before Shinto shrines as a symbol of purity. The most famous of all origami shapes is the flap-winged lucky crane. In strings of a thousand, these are considered a potent charm.

student movement of the 1960s, and the atrocities committed by the terrorist Red Army in the 1970s. Yet again, even revolt tends to take a strangely conformist twist, with rebels forming close-knit groups rather than acting alone.

The modern Madame Butterfly

Despite the post-war emancipation of women, this is still a man's society. The Japanese are fastidiously hygienic, yet men think little, for example, of urinating in the street after a few drinks; moreover, they have no tradition of social gallantry, and will often take a seat while their wives stand, in a way that can seem positively uncouth to Western eyes. The three Confucian obligations on women were, 'Obey your father now, your husband when it shall be decided, and your elder son later on.' Confucius reckoned without the mother-in-law, a formidable figure in many traditionally-run homes.

Large numbers of women now go to university, but most aim to find a husband before the ripe old age of 25. Those who fail can always hope for an arranged

Japanese schoolchildren participate in a mass calligraphy contest at the start of each new year. The events are popular, and stimulate a sense of national identification. The manual dexterity and unusual powers of visual perception of many Japanese workers may be partly attributable to the demands made upon them early in life in mastering Japan's uniquely complex written language. Children need to learn at least 2000 kanji *– pictographs representing different concepts or objects – together with two distinct phonetic alphabets. To read and write fluently calls for extreme mental agility and finely-tuned conditioned reflexes.*

Like so much of Japan's cultural borrowing from the West, these uniforms have a distinctively Japanese touch.

match. Perhaps 40 per cent of Japanese marriages are still arrived at by arrangement rather than through romance, even though nowadays there is no compulsion on couples to accept the dictates of the match-making *omiai*. The Japanese divorce rate is a fraction of that in the West, which must say something for arranged marriages, and even a number of westernised Japanese women tend to defend the practice. 'It helps young people to make a rational choice – and love can follow,' is a typical comment.

Mihoko Goto, a woman in her 30s, says she is deeply disconcerted by the manner in which Westerners seem obsessed by the word 'love', and need to keep asking one another, 'Do you love me?' In Japan, such things are not to be spoken: 'I remember one evening, back from work, my father was sitting on his mat watching TV; my mother, without being asked, brought him a cup of tea. He said, "I was not conscious of it, but I really wanted that tea." That is how one says "I love you" in Japan.'

Japan has the world's highest literacy rate, and schooling is extremely rigorous and competitive – right from kindergarten which starts at the tender age of one. A mother's prime task is to motivate her child to

French critic Roland Barthes called Japan 'the empire of signs'. Tokyo's neon jungle glows with enticements to relax and spend.

study hard enough through middle and high school to gain admittance to one of the top universities, where entry is strictly meritocratic, thus allowing those even from the poorest backgrounds to make good. Reaching one of these unversities is an important step, for that is where the great corporations do their recruiting. Every mother's dream is to see her son become a *sarariman* – a salary man, one of the body of professionals propelling the Japan Inc. juggernaut. There is a price to pay for this pressurised system, however. Failure to win through brings a considerable stigma – and suicide is not infrequent, especially among young people.

The family firm

Sarariman bunka – salary-man culture – is the Japanese equivalent of the Western rat race in pursuit of middle-class security and status symbols, but with one big difference. Joining a major Japanese company is something akin to getting married; it is a lifetime commitment on both sides. The recruit is treated like a new family member, a recently acquired son-in-law, or even a bride come to settle in her husband's home. However bright they may be, the recruits all start at the bottom of a salary 'escalator' that is geared to years of service; bonuses can frequently be good, and the staff are as safe and secure as the company is – no more, no less.

Such corporate togetherness has played a pivotal role in the economic miracle of a people to whom the fulfilment of duty and obligation are as much the object in life as the elusive 'pursuit of happiness' is in the West. Corporation and individual become as one. Each morning at Nissan, for example, after calisthenics

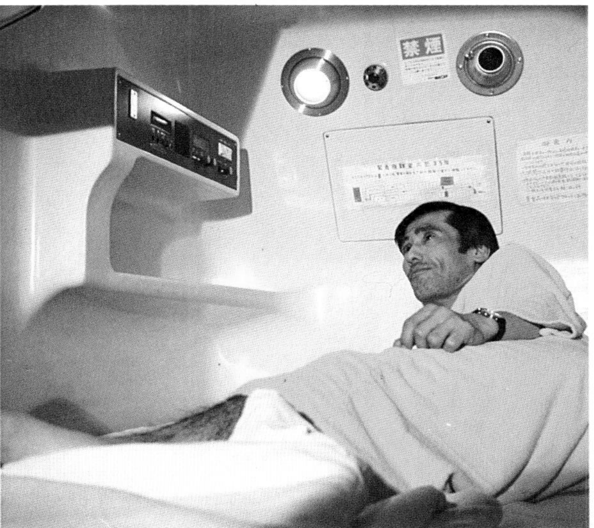

Space is the most precious commodity in Tokyo. Here is one solution: the capsule hotel, in which plastic cocoons substitute for rooms.

Now where did I put it? Tokyo is too congested to make driving practical, and parking even a bicycle is a hazardous affair.

performed to music, workers gather around their foremen to discuss the day's schedule, some new production technique, or whatever else might improve productivity. Only then does work start.

Some big firms begin with a morning ceremony in which the company creed is recited, and the company anthem sung. Motivation may even extend to group meditation in a Buddhist temple, with breaks for calligraphy and fencing practice. In such an enviroment, industrial unrest is deeply embarrassing. As one union leader explains, 'Striking generates within us a sense of shame, for it is not honourable to quarrel within a family.' To save face, workers may wear headbands that indicate their discontent, but at the same time they continue to work while the union and management negotiate. Nevertheless, token strikes are a feature of wage-bargaining each year.

Industry's samurai

The Japan Union of Scientists and Engineers distributed to thousands of businesses a manual titled *Circles of Quality*. The crux of the message it contained was this: 'It is a very poor workshop where the workers are treated as mere cogs in the machinery. The human mind was made to think. A workshop should be a place where people are encouraged to think and to use their know-how.'

What would probably be empty words in a Western business environment is daily reality in Japan. Managing in the Japanese view is based on dialogue and concensus (*ringi*), and when a decision is to be taken, it is considered incorrect, even offensive, not to consult extensively with those in the workforce who will in due course have to implement it. The president of Seiko explains: 'In the West, a decision is an answer to a question. In Japan, it is an understanding of the question. Concensus is the way of achieving that understanding. If we know where the problem lies, it is easy to find the solution.'

In Japan, the top always consults the bottom. This procedure takes more time, but has advantages: above all, that once a decision is taken, its implementation is as swift and as sure as the slash of a *samurai* sword. Such absolute dedication to a cause or course of action goes to Japan's cultural roots. No historic tale thrills the Japanese more than that of the 47 loyal *samurai*, who in 1703 avenged their master's death, knowing that each must pay with his own life.

In his book on Tokyo, the Italian sociologist Fosco Maraini vividly describes meeting one of the great business bosses (*sacho*) in his palatial office: 'Finally,

Tokyo's 100 public swimming pools are crammed to capacity on summer weekends, but no one would consider shirking his duty on weekdays. The Japanese get few holidays, and some are loath to take even those, although this is slowly changing under government pressure.

Entire assembly lines are robot-run in Japan's highly automated car plants. The robots are given affectionate first names, or are named after popular female singing stars. Japan leads the world in robotics. Unions are wary, but accept the principle.

after what seemed an eternity, a door slid open and there was the Great One in his executive suite. He was squatting on a carpet, serenely occupied in painting bamboo leaves!

'Mr Omura seemed completely relaxed. But then he is a man who presents many different faces – sometimes haggard and intense, sometimes silent, thoughtful and rather unnerving, sometimes extrovert, smiling and exuding a certain boyish charm. At all times, however, like every *sacho* of high rank, he wears a charismatic halo and enjoys an advantage that scarcely any president or chairman in the Western world can hope to obtain. Men at his level are virtually the new *daimyo* lords of our age – 20th-century equivalents of the 16th-century feudal barons ...

'Today they are Captains of Industry, trustees for the the firm's success, leading the ever-loyal employees in pursuit of a wider world market, a larger slice of the Gross National Product. The methods and the aims have changed; the status of the man within the social structure remains basically the same.'

A pattern of islands

For all the astonishing changes that have taken place in Japan since the Second World War, parts of the country beyond the main island Honshu remain surprisingly little touched. From Hokkaido in the north to Okinawa in the Japanese-owned Ryukyu Islands far to the south lie areas off the beaten track where rural life continues relatively undisturbed by the influence of industry and social change.

The most outstanding example is Hokkaido, the second largest island, accounting for 21 per cent of the country's land area. It is often regarded as Japan's equivalent of the American West. Until the late 19th century it was more or less ignored by the rest of the country and left to its native inhabitants, the Ainu people, a race of hunters and fishermen who carried on centuries-old patterns of life amidst the island's dazzlingly beautiful landscape of forests, snow-covered volcanic mountains, limpid lakes, hot springs and boiling mud pools.

Then came a government initiative to encourage immigration to Hokkaido. Thousands moved there from the south, rapidly swamping the Ainu, of whom only a handful of full-blooded descendants now survive. Even so, the island preserved its distinctive character. Cities were built for the new arrivals – notably the capital Sapporo, laid out with the help of American architects in the 1870s in a grid of wide, tree-lined avenues – and just over a century later, in 1988, the $33^{1}/_{2}$-mile Seikan railway tunnel was completed to link the island with Honshu. But Hokkaido's countryside (much of which is now enclosed in national parks) remains largely untamed – despite annual influxes of hikers in summer and skiers in winter. Deer and (*continued on p.47*)

Deliciously deceptive: for your eyes only, this three-dimensional menu of imitation dishes is typical of the displays in many of Tokyo's 237,000 eating spots. Plastic food has become a modern folk craft in Japan.

Pachinko, *a vertical pin-ball game with prizes, has long been a drug to Japanese of all ages. Blank-faced addicts stand elbow-to-elbow in one of the country's 16,500* pachinko *parlours. The noise that these machines create is deafening.*

The Geisha, orchid of sex objects

In Kyoto, at nightfall, a lantern beckons discreetly from the alley leading to the *ochaya*, a wooden house in the most refined style, from which waft the muted sounds of the *shamisen.* A swift, light step, the rustle of silk kimono, and she appears: starkly powdered white face with peek-a-bow mouth darkly rouged, brown enamel eyes rimmed in pink, heavy black coiffure precariously burdening so slim a neck.

The geisha is the orchid of sex objects, an exotic creature even in Japanese eyes. Like caviar, she is an acquired and most expensive taste. She wears nightingale droppings (the face mask) which expose just the nape of the neck (the erogenous zone of choice for *samurai* sophisticates); and her beauty is not the kind which seeks to lure the playboys of the Western world. The word geisha means 'cultured person', and that means strictly Japanese culture. There are perhaps a thousand true geisha left in all of Kyoto and Tokyo.

Geisha are ladies of the evening, not the night, and so were unaffected in 1957 when prostitution was outlawed in Japan. Geisha provide ultra-high-status feminine company, never casual sex. Almost all have a regular patron or lover, and some become the mistress of a rich businessman or politician; yet uniquely in Japanese culture, geisha must never marry. Training in the arts of classical Japanese music and dance usually starts at the age of 7 or 8. At 18, the *maiko* (apprentice) achieves the grade of 'sake pourer', and may serve and dance, but not yet converse. At graduation, she selects a professional name, often that of some flower, and begins a lifetime rendezvous with wealth and power. Geisha parties are mainly the preserve of big business, and many deals are concluded with the help of the witty, warming prattle that is their stock-in-trade. Most ordinary Japanese males never have the opportunity to meet a geisha, but her modern counterpart, the bar hostess, is available in abundance: there are perhaps 100,000 in Tokyo alone.

In Kyoto, a doll comes alive as a calligraphic ink known as sumi *is deftly applied to a base of powdered oyster shell.*

Rolls of dyed silk are spun out to dry on a pebble beach. In the land that has catapulted to the vanguard of high technology, crafts thrive using ancient techniques.

wild bears still roam the forests; the mountain streams are still full of fish. As for the people: they retain much of the pioneering spirit of their ancestors. They are well known for being more individualistic than other Japanese, and less burdened by tradition.

Lying off Honshu's southern coast, meanwhile, are the islands of Shikoku and Kyushu. Shikoku is famous for the 88 temples dedicated to Kobo Daishi, also known as Kukai, one of the best-loved of Japan's Buddhist saints. Born on Shikoku in AD 774, he founded the Shingon sect (which still has over 7 million followers in Japan) and also did much to encourage Japanese art and literature as well as championing the importance of public education. Pilgrims who make the journey across the Inland Sea to Shikoku and do the rounds of the 88 temples, praying at each, are said to be set free from the cycle of rebirth when they die. But even for the non-believer the trip is well worth the effort. A range of mountains rising well over 6000 feet forms the island's backbone, furrowed on both sides with steep-sided valleys and dramatically plunging ravines. Tucked into the valleys are small, remote villages where life seems scarcely to have changed since the time of the *shoguns*.

He may keep some of his pigments in instant coffee jars, but this artist creating a kakemono *hanging silk scroll is true to a tradition stretching back a thousand years. To ensure their continuance, the most outstanding craftsmen in dozens of disciplines are honoured as* ningen kokuho, *which translates as 'living national treasures'. In return for government support, a living treasure directs training of the next generation.*

The lush subtropical island of Kyushu is nearer the centre of things ... and always has been. It has a number of important industrial cities, of which Nagasaki had the unpleasant distinction of receiving the second American atomic bomb in 1945. Lying close to Korea and the Asian mainland, it was long the main channel through which outside influences reached Japan. Buddhism and the Chinese system of writing both arrived first in Kyushu, as did Christianity when Portuguese missionaries sailed into Nagasaki's harbour in the mid-16th century. When Japan closed its doors to the outside world in 1637, Dejima island in Nagasaki Bay was the one place in the empire where a few favoured foreign traders were allowed to base themselves. Nagasaki, spread attractively over a series of hills around its bay, is still the most westernised of Japanese cities. It has several 19th-century churches, including the Oura Cathedral dedicated to 26 Christian martyrs crucified in 1597, and a number of handsome mansions and gardens laid out by 19th-century European merchants.

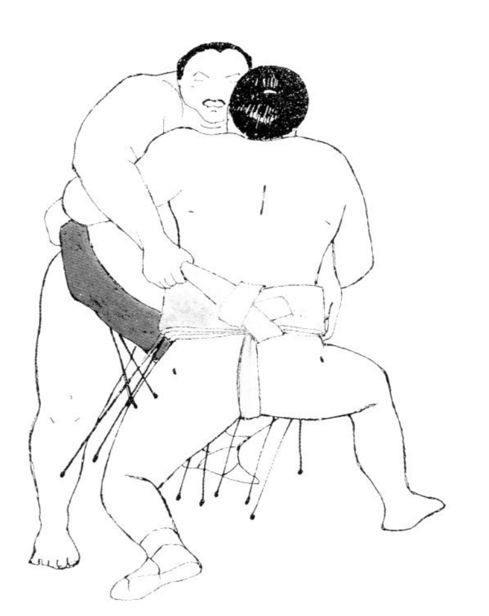

The Ryukyu Islands are another world again, a chain of 55 smaller islands and islets stretching some 750 miles south-west of Kyushu across the East China Sea as far as Taiwan. Small-scale fishing and farming are the chief industries here, though villagers also produce traditional lacquerware and pots.The Ryukyuans are closely related to the Japanese, but have their own language and for many centuries had their own kingdom. Later they came under Chinese and then Japanese domination, and were formally integrated into Japan in 1879. The main island Okinawa is chiefly famous for being the scene of some of the fiercest fighting between the Japanese and Americans in the Second World War. Between March and June 1945 it was bombed, invaded and finally overrun by American troops – who were thus able to establish airbases close to the Japanese mainland. After the war, the islands were put under American control and the entire group was only restored to Japan in 1971.

Hot and steaming, and reaching almost into the tropics, the Ryukyu Islands are a far cry from the icy fastnesses of Hokkaido. With their largely village culture, they are a yet further cry from the urban jungle of Tokyo and the big cities of Honshu. They testify graphically to the diversity that Japan, the most homogenous of nations, still manages to encompass.

The extraordinary resilience of Japanese culture is exemplified by the new-found success of Sumo wrestling. Usurped as the national sport by baseball (a consuming Japanese passion), Sumo has made a comeback, and is gaining an unexpected world-wide following, thanks to television. Sumo goes to the core of Japanese culture and history, yet its explosive bursts of action, interspersed with tension-building preliminaries, make it an ideal TV sport. Sumo dates back to prehistory, when contests were dedicated to the rice gods, and it is choc-a-bloc with Shinto ritual. Before each fight, the wrestlers bow, clap hands to attract the attention of the gods, stamp the ground to drive off any demons and throw purifying salt into the air. There are about 700 professional sumotori *all aspiring to become a* yokozuna, *supreme champion. They are apprenticed at 15 and devote years to gorging on high-calorie food to increase their bulk. Weighing from 300 to 500 pounds, they leap across the tiny ring, each seeking to push or throw the other out, though a knock-down is good enough. A bout is often over in 10 seconds, and it rarely lasts more than a minute, while tournaments (basho) last 15 days.*

Vietnam, Laos and Cambodia

Few countries have suffered more in the second half of the 20th century than Vietnam, Laos and Cambodia. The hell of the Vietnam War affected all three, and for Cambodia there was the further horror of Pol Pot's insane dictatorship. Yet they are also beautiful lands, more gardens than jungles, where for centuries people lived alongside each other in harmony. Now these traditions are beginning to reassert themselves, as their people pick up the old ways of life: planting rice, sewing sarongs, selling fish, praying to Buddha and arranging their children's marriages.

Previous page:
The imagery of tradition and Communism intertwine in this festival scene in Hanoi. The young women are wearing the ao dai *national costume of Vietnam. Their determined expressions are a demonstration of what the French dubbed the Vietnamese 'force tranquille'.*

Big-bellied boats bring rice, fruit and vegetables from the delta lands to the markets of Saigon (Ho Chi Minh City). The voyage is short and highly profitable now that private trading is legal.

Vietnam: The Land of Tight-Lipped Smiles

The very name has become synonymous with war. For more than 30 years, Vietnam was a battlefield, and most of its people grew to adulthood with war as their central experience, and carnage, terror, bombing, dislocation their daily lot. There are people here whose bodies are living museums of 20th-century warfare. See that scar: that's a Japanese bayonet thrust from 1945; those little lumps are French shrapnel collected in 1954; that furrow is the track of a bomb pellet from an American B-52, circa 1972.

Never a lack of heroes...

Vietnam is where the United States determined to stem the tide of Communism in the developing world. It was a fateful choice. The Vietnamese had struggled successfully for 2000 years against absorption by the Chinese, and they had just thrown off a century of French rule when the Americans moved in, not comprehending the extent to which Communism had become identified with nationalism in the years of fighting the French.

There are no more determined, persistent and tenacious people anywhere. Their attitude of mind, with its stress on *dau tranh*, 'struggle', springs from the tough circumstances of their origins around the delta of the Red River, where floods, droughts and typhoons posed as persistent a threat as conquest by their giant neighbour to the north. The Chinese at one stage felt confident enough to name the country Annam, which means the 'pacified south', but that was 1300 years ago, and an example of strictly wishful thinking. 'We have our own mountains and our own rivers, our own customs and traditions,' ran a Great Proclamation of the 15th century. 'We have sometimes been weak and sometimes powerful, but never have we suffered from a lack of heroes.'

The United States spent 140,000 million dollars, dropped 17 million tons of bombs, lost 58,022 killed, and 303,000 injured, before withdrawing in self-disgust. About 4 million Vietnamese, 10 per cent of the population, were killed or injured. On the morning of April 30, 1975, not many minutes after the last Americans had been evacuated by helicopter from their Saigon embassy roof, a Communist tank punched through the gates of the Presidential Palace and a Viet Cong flag was unfurled from the balcony; the country was made whole once more, on maps at least.

Across Thud Ridge

Vietnam snakes around the eastern flank of what was French Indochina; it is slightly larger than Italy and slightly smaller than Japan. The Vietnamese liken it in shape and content to a bamboo pole with a basket of rice on either end. The rice basket in the north is the Red River Delta; that in the south is the Mekong Delta: together, they form two enormous sieves, holding back the rich silt that pours down from the Himalayas. The

Saigon's book market takes place in a street of balconied French colonial houses. Under these awnings, surprising finds of rare and beautiful books may be made. For all its martial reputation, the scholar ranks far above the soldier in traditional Vietnamese society. The literacy rate is high, and the population may be the best educated of any very poor country.

bamboo pole, a green sliver between mountain and sea, hardly 30 miles across, was snapped in two (temporarily, it was supposed) by the 1954 Geneva Accords that saw the exit of the French after their shattering defeat at Dien Bien Phu in the far north. The Vietnam War was concerned with putting the pieces together again – on Communist terms – but it was a hollow achievement. Vietnam, which had been poor, became poorer: a country with the world's fourth-largest army and an average income less than India's.

The national slogan is *Doc Lap, Tu Do, Hanh Phuc* – Independence, Freedom, Happiness – and it is attributed to Ho Chi Minh, the inspirational father-figure to generations in revolt. Bac Ho – Uncle Ho – who received his political training in Stalin's Moscow, became North Vietnam's first president in 1954. He died in office in 1969, and his fate is in a way a metaphor for what happened to his revolution. He lived simply, and asked in his will to be cremated, but instead his body lies embalmed in a marble mausoleum in the capital Hanoi.

The flight from Bangkok into Hanoi follows the route of the American warplanes over mountains the pilots called Thud Ridge. These same pilots are welcomed back now (like Americans in general) and sometimes cannot believe their eyes. The hail of flak and SAM missiles has cleared, as if from a dream, to reveal a timeless pastoral landscape of villages set amidst rice paddies and surrounded by thick clumps of bamboo. Ox-carts trundle slowly around the airport perimeter and, with the ubiquitous squeaky bicycle, set the pace of life. The road to the capital is crowded with peasants driving pigs and ducks, and with the endless stream of bicycles, some carrying two or three people and some bearing incredible loads of rice, charcoal or livestock. Out on the paddies, women rhythmically swing baskets on strings to slop water from one field to the next, and men carry baskets of fertiliser: pig excrement and chopped leaves are best, so it is said.

A 'harvest of life deeply rooted in the harvest of rice,' is how William Broyles, a former American combat officer, described what he found when he returned to Vietnam some years after the war. 'It seemed incredible,' he wondered, 'that this backward place could have taken those boys riding on the backs of water buffalo and made them anti-aircraft gunners and platoon commanders, and could have organised them to build and maintain a vast logistical network across more than 3500 miles of trackless mountain and jungle, could have found ways to defeat every new technological weapon we developed. It simply didn't compute.'

One look at Hanoi, and the wonder grows. It is as though a sleepy French provincial town of 50 years ago has been levitated through time and space. Scattered lakes enhance the crumbling charm of its shady boulevards and low colonial buildings adorned with green shutters. Most enchanting is the Lake of the Returned Sword (Vietnam's equivalent of King Arthur was a 15th-century emperor), with a tiny pagoda perched on an islet in the middle. A red star tops the pagoda, much as Communism was planted on top of the existing culture – itself a complex fusion of all the great philosophies of the East. 'The Vietnamese never throw

Crops cover some of the scars of war in Hue, the old imperial capital on the Perfume River. This is one of ten gates to the Citadel, where 10,000 people died during ferocious fighting in 1968. Lack of funds means that typhoons and creeping vegetation continue the process of dilapidation.

anything away, so they've simply placed each new bureaucracy on top of the one before,' a Western diplomat told Broyles. 'The French bureaucracy was laid over the Confucian bureaucracy, and the Communist over that. It's impossible to figure out. Even the Vietnamese don't understand how it works.'

In 1986, even the ageing Communist mandarins admitted that it was not working at all well, and a momentous Party congress legalised private enterprise – without, of course, throwing away anything of the existing system.

Tet: horror and hope

Along the Ben Hai River is where the country broke: for 10 years this was a free-fire zone between north and south and the focus of ferocious fighting. Now sampans drift lazily between the rice paddies, past the occasional boy on a buffalo and beside women wading in the shallows to gather oysters. In the verdant, misty hills, resettled with hill-tribe villages, are the dwindling remains of the Rockpile, Hamburger Hill, Firebase Ripcord, Khe Sanh and other American strongpoints, worried over by scrap-hunters. Vietnam leads the world in scrap metal. In places, the ground is carpeted with spent rounds, and some that are still live, and the war continues to take its toll.

Southwards along the green corridor between lovely waterfall-spouting mountains and the coast, chattering schoolchildren trot down paths where US Marine patrols were ambushed, and rice dries on roads once churned up by tank tracks. Areas of bare red earth and piles of scrap collected for recycling are all that is now left of a vast American civilisation, of camps, depots, airfields, movie theatres, ice-cream parlours ... Ice cream, in fact, is one American innovation that endures to this day; called *kem*, it is often served attractively in baby coconuts.

Hue, the old imperial capital on the Perfume River, is where Vietnam stores its soul. The accent is softer than elsewhere, the women (everyone insists) more beautiful. It has been said that 'grief smiles and joy sighs' in Hue. A 3000 verse poem commemorates the sack of the city by the French in 1885, when the palace was cleaned out to the last toothpick, and the imperial library burned for three days. Seventy years later, the area around Hue was laid waste during the war that drove out the French, and the poets were kept busy once more, but so far they have been unable to find words for what happened during the 1968 Tet Offensive, when the city was seized by the Communists and pounded to bits in the course of its gradual recapture.

The bits have been patched together again. The *Dai Noi* (Imperial Enclosure) is in recognisable shape, and incense burns once more before the city's guardian

The conical hat of Vietnam is a very effective umbrella as well as sun-shade. The best are said to be made around Hue.

These two girls in the market of Haiphong, Hanoi's port on the Gulf of Tonkin, had nothing but a few flowers to sell. Many here have joined the exodus of 'boat people' who risked storms, pirates and foreign internment to seek a new life abroad.

images in Thien Mu (Heavenly Lady) Pagoda, on the spot where, so it is said, a heavenly vision appeared to direct its founding. The incense is thickest during Tet, another word made ugly by war, and now on the mend. Tet is the Vietnamese New Year, and its most joyous time of celebration. On the evening of Tet, every pagoda in the country is an aromatic smokestack filled with people waving incense sticks before the gilded Buddha images.

'Tet is everyone's birthday, the holiday of holidays, an occasion to meditate the past, to enjoy the present, and to contemplate the future,' explains Vietnamese writer Tran Van Dinh. 'It embodies the entire spectrum of Vietnamese mythology and religion, the whole concept of man and woman and their relationship to the dead and the living and the spirits.' For Tet, all the family gets together – and this being Vietnam, all the family means not only the living generation, but all the ancestors as well. First comes the end-of-year dinner, when the ancestors are invited back to join in the celebrations and reunions, and horoscopes are cast. At midnight, the entire country erupts with firecrackers, and the crackle and bang carries on until morning when a bluish haze greets the dawn. The idea is to drive off the evil spirits – 'to make everything unhappy go away'. Then comes the visiting, and eating. 'Hungry all year – Tet three days full' is an old saying that has gained poignant new meaning.

The Street of the Popular Uprising

Saigon is still Saigon, to the exasperation of Party ideologues, yet also the country's mainspring and its commercial hub. Only on Government documents, and airline tickets, does it go by its new, official name, Ho Chi Minh City. While austere, puritanical Hanoi lives by the rules, Saigon lives by its wits, as much now as ever.

Rice keeps Vietnam alive, but a post-war baby boom and a series of disastrous floods, droughts and typhoons keep straining resources. So does the country's economic plight. Vietnam is said to trade its best rice for inferior grain in order to acquire desperately needed foreign exchange.

What once was elegant Catinat Street under the French – Saigon's equivalent of the Champs Elysées – became carousing Freedom Street (Tu Do) in the American era, and is now Dong Khoi, The Street of the Popular Uprising. Nowadays, its wild bars have become antique shops, but do not be misled by looks. Saigon is a city of desperate, inventive enterprise in which more than 3 million people claw for a living any way they can. There are, for example, the bicycle tyre repairmen squatting at every corner, with a water basin, a packet of patches and a rusty air pump at the ready. On top of the heap are the 'resellers' who traffic in luxury goods that materialise in all sorts of ways.

Tran Bach Dang, the city's underground Communist commander in the war, has gone on to write popular spy novels. Like many other Viet Cong veterans, he frets over post-war failure, and what went wrong. For such people, it is easy to blame Hanoi. As for the glum, tight-fisted Russians who for a long time prowled the streets, they proved a poor substitute for the free-spending Americans. '*Lien Xo*' is what the children shout at whites; it means Russian – the only kind of white most of them know. A handy phrase to remember is '*Khong phai Lien Xo*' – 'I am not a Russian'. Eyes light up if it is an American, for the *do la*, the American dollar, has prevailed where force of arms failed.

From the finest French champagne to Russian caviar, every luxury is available in the back rooms of little shops at astoundingly low prices – in dollars. Only dollars, at a substantially less generous rate, are accepted in the Saigon-Intershop Supermarket, a joint venture between the Government and Singapore traders which was intended to soak up some of the hard currency generated by the *Viet Kieu* – the hundreds of thousands of Vietnamese living abroad. These expatriates in France, the United States and Australia send their relatives consumer goods, not so much to use as to sell on the most open black market in the world. In the markets and on the streets of Saigon, everything is for sale.

The scramble has begun to sort out a new privileged class, the children of successful entrepreneurs, and of high Party officials whose puritanical idealism may have begun to wear thin. They can be seen in clusters every Sunday evening, revving their little Suzuki and Honda buzzbikes down Dong Khoi Street in the cheerful social ritual that has come to be known as *chay rong rong*, the big ride-around. Another interesting symbol for the survival of old ways is the Catholic cathedral at the top of Dong Khoi, which still has three masses daily.

This Chinese-style dragon with five claws was the emblem of Vietnam's emperors. Vietnam's love-hate relationship with China goes back 2000 years – the more it absorbed Chinese culture, the more it fought to be free.

Fish ranks second to rice as Vietnam's most important staple food, but freshwater yields have dropped in some areas due to pollution. Exacerbating the problem is the loss of thousands of boats taken by refugees.

The cranes of heaven

The Vietnam War added a new word to the English language: ecocide – the destruction of the environment for military purposes. To flush out the enemy, the US waged war on nature, bulldozing, bombing and flaming forests, and spraying toxic chemicals to destroy all vegetation. In this way, 8000 square miles of forest and farmland were lost, and the war left in its wake widespread erosion and a severely depleted wildlife. Other noxious after-effects ranged from plagues of rodents to 'bomb crater malaria'.

This was all the more a tragedy because Vietnam is an exceptionally beautiful country. With landscape ranging from the long and suitably palm-fringed beaches around Vung-tau not far from Saigon in the south, to the coconut plantations of Cantho and Ca-mau, to the Hoa-binh mountains south-west of Hanoi, it can claim to be Asia in miniature. The South offers lush tropical vegetation, the luxuriant gardens of Saigon and the jungles of the Mekong Delta; in the north are impenetrable forests and the immense stretches of rice fields around Hanoi ... in short, a palette of greens encompassing every conceivable shade. In some areas the landscape takes on unique shapes as well as colours. One of the most astonishing is the Bay of Along in the far north, near the Chinese frontier. Here, hills and mountains rising sheer from the sea spread out for miles on every side, forming a huge congregation of black and rocky outcrops which resemble nothing so much as an army of petrified giants guarding the border.

Another exceptional landscape is that of the Mekong Delta. Its mangrove swamps and reed beds suffered worst at the hands of the Americans, and a once-lush green landscape became a silent, grey mass of dead plants. One of many incidental casualties was the Eastern Sarus Crane; a symbol of fidelity, longevity and good luck, this is the bird which according to myth is sent from heaven to fetch those destined for eternal life. The Mekong's Plain of Reeds had been its last refuge, and when the war came, the cranes vanished forever, it was feared.

Today the delta is making a comeback, the sea flushing away the poisons faster than in other places, and it is again a major rice producer. In 1985, a farmer reported spotting what he thought was a crane. Two years later, more than 100 were counted; in 1989, more than 400; and by 1990, there were 1000 or more. The cranes of heaven had returned to Vietnam.

The barrels contain nuoc-mam, *a pungent fish sauce that is to Vietnamese cooking what soy sauce is to Japanese. It is made by a fermentation process that takes up to a year.*

This child is special – she is a member of the first generation of Vietnamese in 50 years to have no experience of the horrors of war.

At harvest time, Vietnam is carpeted with rice drying in the sun – on roadsides, in backyards or, as here, on sheets of canvas. The country has hardly any agricultural machinery.

The rice pancakes drying on a fine straw mesh will be filled with minced pork and mushrooms, and served with a special sauce.

Vietnam has an exciting, varied cuisine, even if nowadays most people are reduced to simple dishes such as pho – noodle soup.

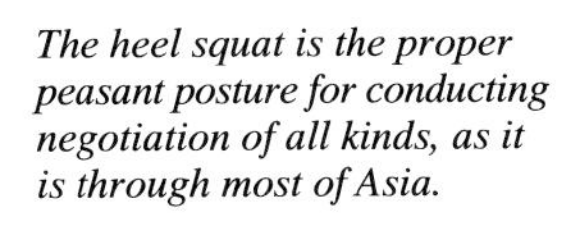

The heel squat is the proper peasant posture for conducting negotiation of all kinds, as it is through most of Asia.

Laos: Land of the Million Elephants

Hmong villages command the mountain heights of northern Laos. In this fastness – remote enough for a major power to wage war in secret – a substantial portion of the world's opium is grown.

Sail up the Mekong and eventually you come to Laos. There are no roads to speak of, and until 1990 Laos was linked to the Western world by a single telephone line. The population can only be guessed at, but it is less than 4 million, spread across an area larger than that of Britain – if you can imagine Britain as a rugged, tropical fastness of teakwood forest and tiger trails. 'One of Asia's most undeveloped and undiscovered countries ... an unparalleled glimpse of old South-East Asia,' extols one of the very few modern guidebooks to address Laos and its peculiar wonders.

The Kingdom of the Million Elephants and White Parasol was the country's majestic formal title until the events of 1975, and Western travellers tended to be no less lyrical in their romantic assessments of its charms. The novelist Jean Larteguy captured the sentiment in

his book *The Bronze Drum*, in which he had his character Gibelin declare:

'That's why I love this country: because of certain encounters that have something miraculous about them ... on the river ... in the forest, in the distant isolated valleys, in the blue highlands of the Meos when the whole of the Trans Ninh is one vast flower-bed. I've come across men in their pure state, living in natural surroundings that haven't yet been spoiled. It's difficult to explain, but now I feel almost inflated with gratitude towards this country which has given me so much delight ... it's paradise ... the women's amber bodies clad in gold and silver cloth! The *khene* music! The girls bathing naked in the red rivers, the feast days, the courts of love, the *bonzes* ...'

These words were published in 1967, when the outside world was unaware that the distant valleys and blue highlands were being carpet-bombed. More than 2 million tons of bombs were eventually dropped on Laos; this is a third more in tonnage than the United States dropped on Nazi Germany, and three times the amount used in the Korean War. Laos has the unlikely distinction of being the most heavily bombed country, per capita, in the history of warfare.

The quest for New Lao Man

What the American pilots called Thud Ridge makes up most of Laos; that and the long upper stretch of the Mekong flood plain. Steep mountains rib the north of the country, and in their midst is the Plain of Jars, a part of the Plateau de Xiangkhoang. This is the core of mainland South-East Asia, a wedge between all of its major civilisations, and consequently on the line of march of every conqueror from the dawn of history. Laos is at the crossroads of war paths, a natural battleground, and as such it was inevitably sucked into the wider Vietnam conflict, and with much the same outcome.

In 1975, Communist Pathet Lao troops entered the capital Vientiane without firing a shot. On December 2, in the gym of what had been the American school, King Savang Vatthana (whose earliest ancestor is said to have descended to earth by means of a giant liana, like some divine Jack in the Beanstalk) abdicated his throne, and the Kingdom of the Million Elephants

Transport ... tractor ... war chariot ... elephants are the uniquely adaptable heavy vehicles of the Laotian jungles, and valued accordingly. Around the Plain of Jars, a trained elephant is between 6 and 20 times the price of a bride.

became the Lao People's Democratic Republic.

The author Paul Theroux described Vientiane, in its pre-Communist days, as a place where 'the brothels are cleaner than the hotels, marijuana is cheaper than pipe tobacco, and opium easier to find than a cold glass of beer.' The Pathet Lao had survived six years of bombing by living in caves, and were in no mood to party. Vientiane's sleazy-going days were over: bars were closed, a curfew imposed, and girls who used make-up or painted their nails were denounced as *yakhini* – ogres. The new government's grand plan for Laos was a Stalinist system of collectivisation, and as many as 40,000 members of the royalist forces, and others considered most likely to demur, were rounded up and consigned to 're-education camps'.

Modern Laos is a French creation, and the Laotians had no say when their borders were set. The population consists, in roughly equal proportions, of lowland Lao, close kin to the Thais, and as many as 70 other distinct cultures dispersed over the high ground. Out of this ethnic stew, a 'new Lao Socialist man' was supposed to evolve, purified of such elements as 'the depraved culture of the West' and of *ngom ngouai* – primitive superstitions. Buddhism passed muster with the Laotian Marxists, but not *phi* spirit worship, and rites such as animal sacrifice were forbidden as 'backward tendencies which constitute an obstacle to production'. The hill tribes' traditional, but destructive, slash-and-burn method of forest agriculture was also on their hit list.

An estimated 10 per cent of the population was distressed enough by the Pathet Lao programme to flee across the Mekong into Thailand, taking all that they

The Lao people live along the Mekong and its tributaries, following much the same way of life as their cousins, the Thais. Every family has its boat, and every village its wat *(Buddhist temple-monasteries) with at least one resident monk.*

could with them; they included most of the people with something to take. It seemed as though even the earth spirits were in revolt. Drought followed by floods in 1976 was followed, in turn, by a bad drought in 1978, then more floods in 1980. But by then, the creation of new Lao man had been put on hold. Well ahead of liberalisation moves in Moscow, a sort of Pathet Lao *Perestroika* was put into effect in Vientiane; they called it *chintanakan mai* – new thinking.

City of the Moon

Vientiane is what the French cartographers made of Wieng Chan, City of the Moon. It occupies a bend of the Mekong and, seen from above, almost disappears into the tropical foliage. All the regional powers controlled this place at some time during its first 1000 years, and then the French, Americans, and Russians had their say; it shows in little ways. A distinctly French aroma, for example, mingles with the morning mists off the Mekong: fresh-baked baguettes are a Vientiane speciality.

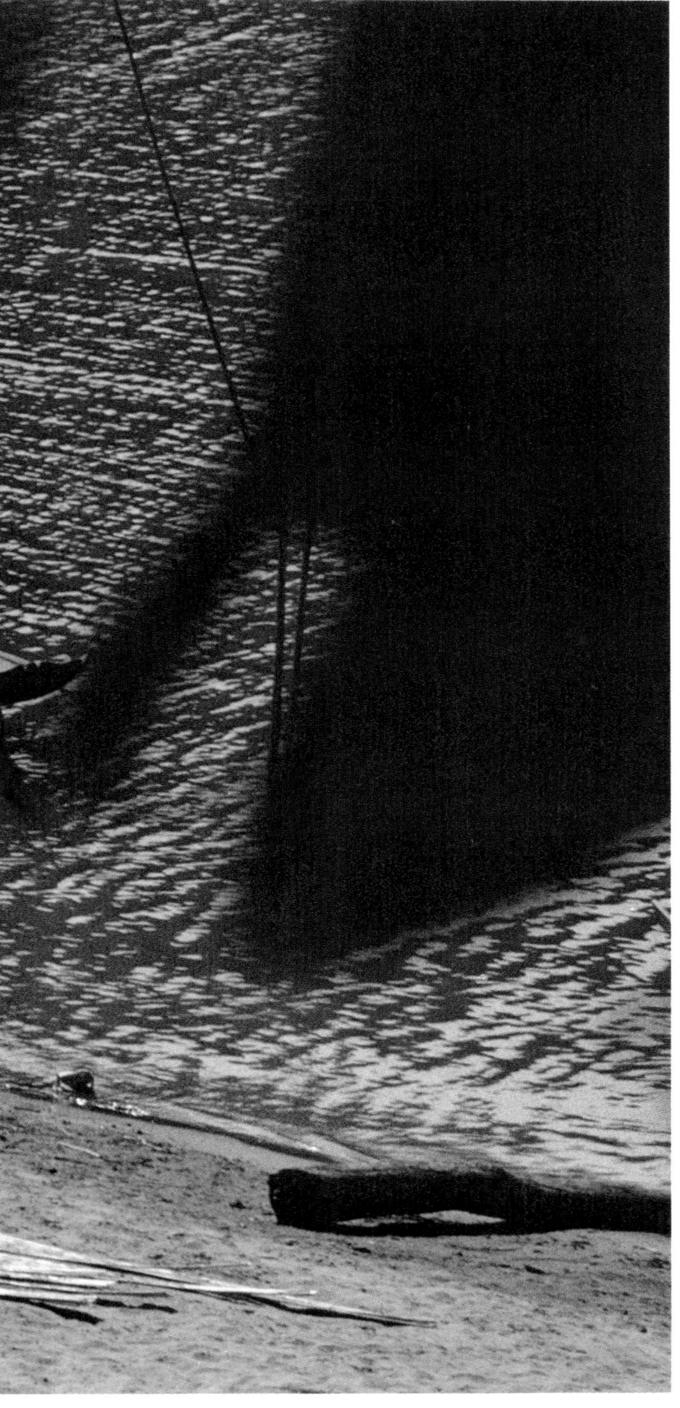

The frogs croaking in the ditches create more of a racket than the trickle of traffic puttering up Thanon Lan Xang (Million Elephants Avenue) to the Victory Gate, a squat, Oriental version of the Arc de Triomphe that turns out to have been built in 1969 with cement donated by the United States for the construction of a new airport. Yet the torpor is lifting. A few years ago, when most shops were as shuttered as the country itself, Vientiane could not boast even a single Laotian restaurant. Now there are plenty of eating places, and discos besides, purveying everything from local *lam wong* rhythms to Western rock, and the dancers no longer have to stay two feet apart, as the Government initially decreed. Without in any way relaxing their political grip, the secretive Pathet Lao did an about-turn, and opened up the country to private enterprise, even while still dutifully berating 'the lackeys of American imperialism'. Strings of Christmas lights were dug out of somewhere to brighten the night, and the Lan Xang Hotel perfectly captured the breezy mood of *chintanakan mai* by erecting a flashing neon hammer and sickle.

The central Morning Market has become a misnomer, now that it bustles all day, with Japanese electronic goods, Thai foods and just about anything else available since restrictions were relaxed. There is no black market, so long as the Lao kip floats free against the Thai baht and American dollar. Nothing could be simpler than the way it was conceived: an employee of the Central Bank strolled through the market each

The rice paddy is the great provider of the Lao, its extra bounty including fish, crabs and a variety of nourishing water plants. Pak ven, *a kind of cress, is being harvested here.*

morning to check what stallholders were offering, and that determined the official exchange rate.

Luang Prabang, the former royal capital, is three days up the Mekong, or 40 minutes by the Anotov 24 turbo-prop, whose arrival in the morning depends upon when the mists lift. Preserved by neglect and isolation, this jumble of pagodas, old French mansions, and stilted bamboo dwellings sustains a rhythm of life from a previous age. Naked children play in the river; water buffalo snooze in the streets; monks make the rounds with their food bowls; peasants lug their produce to market, including such locally appreciated edibles as spiny anteaters, rats, owls, and flying beetles, said to go down well with a beer.

The Royal Palace sits by the river, under a steep, pagoda-dotted hill. It is a French colonial creation with a little Lao in the design, a lot of Versailles, and a crimson throne room with gold trimmings. Nowadays it is a museum. One wing is full of diplomatic gifts, thoughtfully arranged between Capitalist and Socialist, and including a piece of moon rock.

Secrets of the opium poppy

Farther up the Mekong, past the beached carcases of American gunboats and past villages noted for their fiery liquor, the boiling, churning river gradually narrows, and the jungle walls close in. This is the back door into the Golden Triangle – although, at the moment, a closed door. It is legal to cultivate opium in these mountains, and an estimated annual production of 300 tons makes Laos the third-biggest producer after Burma and Afghanistan. A substantial portion is smuggled out through Thailand, some already refined into heroin in jungle laboratories.

Defining the problem is easier than solving it. The Hmong are the major opium cultivators and the dominant tribal power of the mountains: hardy, mettlesome farmer-hunter-warriors who have grown the opium poppy for more than 150 years. Opium is perfect for their needs – a compact cash crop that grows well on the high and remote mountain slopes. It is impervious to any amount of rough handling on long journeys by pack donkey or on a man's back, and it can be readily bartered for the iron that the Hmong need to make their machetes, farming tools and flintlock rifles, and for the silver they cherish as a display and store of wealth. Hmong legends relate how the first poppies grew out of the grave of a beautiful girl, who wanted to relieve the great sorrow of the lover she left behind. Every Hmong child learns the lore and the intricacies of poppy culture and opium extraction as part of its basic education.

In September or October, the small, dark seeds are scattered by hand, then carefully mixed into the soil. The plants are thinned when they reach a few inches, and the leaves eaten as salad. Weeding is a back-breaking task, and the whims of nature are a constant hazard: too many overcast days stunt growth; a sudden hailstorm can smash the delicate buds; an early frost will kill them; and a blundering elephant, or mating tigers, or any other chance incursion by forest beasts can flatten the patch in a few minutes. Harvesting is in late December to early February, when the bulbs range in size from that of a golf ball to a tennis ball, and it involves weeks of exacting toil. Incisions are made in

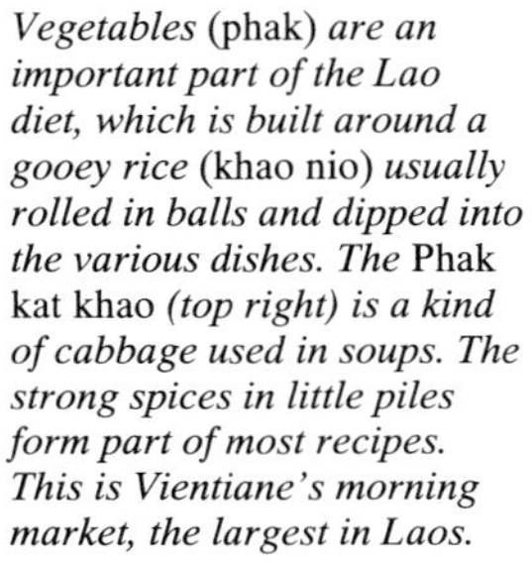

Vegetables (phak) *are an important part of the Lao diet, which is built around a gooey rice* (khao nio) *usually rolled in balls and dipped into the various dishes. The* Phak kat khao *(top right) is a kind of cabbage used in soups. The strong spices in little piles form part of most recipes. This is Vientiane's morning market, the largest in Laos.*

This Kuy family from Southern Laos belongs to one of 50 Lao Theung (Lao of the Slopes) tribes whose ancestors were driven into the hills when the Lao began arriving in the 12th century. Oppressed by the Lao – who referred to them as Kha, or slaves – Lao Theung provided many Communist recruits and, like other mountain peoples, suffered most from the war. All Laotians – Lao, Lao Theung and Lao Soung (Mountain Lao) – are strongly attached to family life, and believe that having many children assures a happy old age.

The Lao house is built on stilts as a protection from wild animals and floods, and to provide some airiness during the hot season. A new husband moves in with the family of his bride until he can build his own home nearby; in this way, families come to occupy mu ban, *or groups of adjacent homes. Basic at first, like the one seen here, homes are enlarged and improved through the years. They are usually bequeathed to the daughter who has cared for her parents in their old age.*

each bulb, and the resin that oozes out overnight is scraped off before the early morning sun has a chance to dry it up. Depending on the size of the bulb, this is repeated several times.

A typical family grows up to an acre of poppies yielding about 20 pounds of smoking opium – enough to maintain itself in relative prosperity if bartered to smugglers. Under pressure from the United States, the Vientiane government is committed to make a 'maximum effort' to stop illicit trafficking, and to convince at least some poppy growers to switch crops, but it has every reason to tread carefully with the fiercely independent Hmong, who are traditionally at odds with the lowland Lao and made up the bulk of the American CIA's secret wartime army.

When the Pathet Lao took over, the Hmong army commander Vang Pao (who became a naturalised American) fled with his six wives and 29 children, and so did tens of thousands of others, but some insurgency continued. By the early 1990s, insurgents and drug smugglers were becoming hard to tell apart.

Old ways that live on...

Despite the antipathy of the Paphet Lao government for many of Laos's old ways, it has never been able to stamp them out completely. One of its first acts on gaining power, for example, was to abolish the traditional Laotian calendar. Accordingly, the country now works to international time-scales, but that does not stop village people and many city dwellers from celebrating a number of the old annual festivals.

Among the most intriguing of these is Pimai, the old New Year, which falls in mid-April. Traditionally, it has been seen as a day that exists in a kind of limbo, belonging neither to the old year nor the new – and consequently as a day in which you are permitted to take the sort of liberties you would not dream of taking at any other time of the year. Women chase men through the villages, armed with buckets full of muddy water; the men reply in kind, while children enjoy their own revels. Soon everyone is soaked. Luckily, it is midsummer, and within an hour they are all dry again.

In May comes a new set of festivities, this time designed to encourage the gods to send the rains that will help the rice crops to grow. The centrepiece of the occasion is a fireworks display with a special phallic symbolism. The rockets carry their 'seed' into the sky where they open and shower down the blessings of fertility. None of this is lost on the spectators who rib each other with ribald jokes and suggestive comments. Often choirs of men and women start singing traditional songs, the different parts of each choir taking it in turn to pick up the refrains. These songs also tend to be suggestive and provoke regular gales of laughter.

There is more to this seemingly timeless scene than meets the eye. Marxism and Buddhism came to terms in Laos, where Party leaders attend major religious festivals and the monks play an important role in education and herbal medicine.

In October the rainy season draws to its end – and with it the Buddhist season of fasts. This lasts three months during which all *bonzes* (monks) are required to be back in their monasteries by nightfall and are only allowed out in the morning to receive their food. The end of the fast is celebrated with canoe races on the Mekong between boats from different villages, districts and even some government ministries. This festival, at least, is encouraged by the Government and a number of Paphet Lao officials come to watch the proceedings from a riverside grandstand – the spirit of competition and emulation required for the races accords perfectly with the Government's ideological lines.

A harvest of bombs

There are places in Laos where the bombs fell thicker than poppy seeds, and where scrap metal – the harvest of war – is now the main, and sometimes only, cash crop. The Plain of Jars, 100 miles north-east of Vientiane, with its high, rolling forests and meadowland sandwiched between green mountains, is renowned for its beauty, its mild climate, and its jars – mysterious pots left by some forgotten civilisation. It is also the age-old invasion route into and out of the Mekong valley, and between Thailand and Vietnam, and as such it became a target of American 'interdiction'.

Hundreds of villages were razed, and by 1969 the Plain was deserted. Phonsavanh, a rickety replacement for Xieng Khwang, the destroyed regional capital, is the scrap metal collection centre where villagers bring the debris they find; they receive the equivalent of 50 American cents a kilo, and the scrap is sold on to Thailand, but there is a price still to pay. Up to ten Plains people a month continue to be killed by *bombi*, which is what the Laotians call the anti-personnel 'pineapple' bomblets scattered from cluster bombs. When the Quakers cleared ground to build a school in 1989, their metal detectors found 18 *bombis*, two medium-sized unexploded bombs and one large bomb that was too deep to dig out – so they built over it.

The bombing was most intense near the Vietnam border, along the constantly shifting Ho Chi Minh Trail that was the Communist supply line into South Vietnam. Climb into these foothills and the scenery changes from diked paddy fields to a rocky moonscape of bomb craters, sometimes with new villages perched around the edges. Bits of downed American aircraft and bomb shards have become support beams for stilt houses, cooking utensils and boats.

Now a new trail crosses the old one – of black market Western goods moving from Thailand, through Laos and into Vietnam.

Each sunrise, the bonzes *(monks) form a line and make the round of the neighbourhood with their food bowls, which are soon filled with freshly-cooked rice. The Government tried to ban begging as unseemly for a Socialist state, but quickly relented in the face of mass protest.*

Hmong girls are commonly weighed down by a heavy load of silver jewellery, which constitutes the family fortune. In times of need, a bangle or bracelet has to be sacrificed. Opium cultivation has given the Hmong relative wealth, but also tribulation. Caught in the war and its aftermath, many fled their mountains. More than 70,000 Hmong now live in California.

Ox-carts plod past a Soviet-supplied Vietnamese tank used in the drive against the Khmer Rouge. The humble track is National Road 5, from Phnom Penh to Battambang (Cambodia's second city) and the Thai border. Cambodia inherited a sparse road network from the French, and 20 years of war and neglect have devastated it.

The black market not only thrives under Cambodia's peculiar 'parallel' economy, but also offers exciting possibilities for recycling, as this home constructed out of smuggled soft drink containers demonstrates.

Cambodia: After the Holocaust

'What is it to die? To survive and suffer is much worse,' mutters the old food peddler squatting on the pavement of Monivong Boulevard in Phnom Penh. The monsoon rain is drumming on the corrugated iron roof of his stand, and drops of warm water are landing on the gooey rice balls wrapped in banana leaves.

Life in Cambodia may not yet be worth living, but the old man's grumbling is confirmation of how things improved under the stern supervision of the Vietnamese. Under the Khmer Rouge, grumblers were shot out of hand, and when the bullets ran short, they got beaten to death.

It is hardly 150 miles from Saigon to Phnom Penh, the Cambodian capital on the lower Mekong, and the Vietnam War spilled over the border just as inevitably as in Laos. There the similarity ended. The Khmer Rouge (Cambodian Reds) had no caves in which to hide, and they acquired a maniacal resolve in five years of creeping advance under saturation bombing. They took Phnom Penh on April 17, 1975, just 13 days before the fall of Saigon. It was Chaul Chnam, the Cambodian New Year, but there was no joy in the eyes of the conquerors, most of whom were very young and clad as peasant warriors, in black, with chequered scarves and leather sandals.

Methodically, they secured the city, then ordered everyone out – even the dying in the fetid hospitals. Other towns were emptied in the same way, and millions of famished and disease-wracked people were sent stumbling through the rice lands and the jungles with neither food nor possessions. They were told that this was Year Zero, and that Angka – the Organisation – would provide for a new future of perfect purity. Then they were put to work in forced labour battalions on huge irrigation sites.

In the 44 months of Khmer Rouge rule, between 1 and 3 million Cambodians perished. Hundreds of thousands were butchered in cold blood, and the rest were killed off by malaria, famine and exposure; the jungle beasts also had their fill. Intellectuals and professionals were a particular target, and just to wear spectacles was to court disaster. A fanatic xenophobia accompanied the whole 'purification' process, and Cambodia's Vietnamese community was massacred. Finally, in the 44th month, Vietnam attacked, captured Phnom Penh, and installed a client regime led by disaffected elements within the Khmer Rouge. This stayed in power for ten years until international efforts to resolve the Cambodian problem began to bear some fruit and led in 1991 to the return of the former king, now known as Prince Sihanouk, as head of state.

The ravaged city's population is back to 700,000, which is more than enough: most are peasant squatters who grabbed their pick of the homes of the dead, and now there is strict influx control. *Cyclos* (pedicabs), bicycles and pony carts rush around the streets, past the shells of burnt-out buildings. Here and there, an official black car, a military vehicle or a jeep with the UNICEF insignia, proceeds with horn blaring. Darting eyes still cast about for long-lost loved ones – more out of habit

Cambodians are not allowed to forget the horrors of their holocaust, as is evident from the gruesome fare on offer in this Phnom Penh cinema. Authentic reminders include a torture centre, which can be viewed much as it was found in 1979, and a 'killing field' ten miles from the city, where thousands of skulls are visible behind glass in a memorial shrine. With the Khmer Rouge still highly active, the Government's policy has been to focus hatred on its predecessor.

than hope – and there is still some desultory treasure-hunting for valuables buried in gardens on the day of the diaspora.

Everything has had to be re-created from almost nothing. Under the Khmer Rouge, formal education was abolished, and so was currency – the Khmer Rouge even blew up the National Bank, and the National Library was turned into a stable, its books scattered in the streets. Only 2724 of the country's 21,611 pre-war schoolteachers were listed as survivors, but nobody evidently took a count of the toll among the 50,000 Buddhist monks, who were all defrocked and forced into labour brigades. Many of the 3000 temples and pagodas were destroyed, or turned into storehouses or prisons, while their Buddha images were smashed or dumped into rivers. Consequently a factory in Phnom Penh is doing a brisk trade in churning out cement Buddhas as emergency replacements. Cambodia also lost 90 per cent of its classical dancers, although a new national troupe is now in training.

The dancers are a last living link with a golden age of 1000 years ago, when the god-kings of Angkor built great temple cities whose magnificent ruins to the north of Phnom Penh are one of the wonders of the world; they include Angkor Wat, the largest religious edifice ever constructed. By a cruel twist, it was Angkor that helped to inspire Pol Pot, the evil genius of the Khmer Rouge. 'If our people can make Angkor, they can make anything,' he enthused in 1977.

The ancient kingdom grew rich and powerful because it had a sophisticated irrigation system that enabled it to produce surpluses of rice – precisely what Pol Pot dreamed of achieving, though he never succeeded. And just like Pol Pot, it depended upon the massive use of forced labour.

The Cambodian countryside bristles with booby-traps, the result of years of indiscriminate mine-laying: Cambodia has the highest proportion of maimed people in the world. The dangers are particularly acute around Angkor, where at one point a situation worthy of an Indiana Jones film developed, with Khmer Rouge infiltrators, the Cambodian army, and robber gangs all playing a deadly game of hide-and-seek among the snake-infested ruins. In a land where government jobs paid the equivalent of three American dollars a month, rapacious dealers in antiquities on the Thai border were said to be offering a kilo of gold for every kilo of exquisite stone carving that remained to be torn from the monuments.

Sugar palms dot the paddy dikes of Cambodia's ricelands and provide the material for housing. The sap is tapped into bamboo buckets and made into wine or vinegar, or boiled down to a brownish paste: Cambodian sugar. For a long time a national symbol, the sugar palm has lately distinguished itself by surviving any amount of damage from shells, shrapnel and stray bullets.

Orphans of the holocaust live in village-like communities and contribute to their upkeep by growing vegetables and rearing livestock. Doctors of the international aid organisations are in regular attendance.

Thailand

Alone among the nations of South-East Asia, Thailand was never colonised by the European powers. As a result, the Thais – their very name means 'free' – have kept alive an exceptional number of their ancient traditions: their unique form of Buddhism, their sinuous classical dances, their glorious architectural heritage. But the rulers whose deft diplomacy held the great powers at bay were also able to profit from the West ... and they still do. Problems abound in this land set in a troubled region, but tourism and a pragmatic economic policy keep it among South-East Asia's more prosperous countries.

The sociable, inquisitive gibbon is easily captured. The small expressive face attracts sympathy, but not enough to soften the hearts of rapacious animal traders, whose activities imperil Thailand's primates.

Thailand has about 5000 working elephants – down from more than 100,000 a century ago, and sure to fall further. An elephant takes five years to train for forestry work. Under Thai law, it is retired at the age of 60 and released to join the few thousand living wild in the country's national parks.

Previous page:
The Thai smile hides great fortitude, nowhere more than in the poor, neglected north-east provinces where tourists rarely stray. For all their gentle manner, Thai women are resourceful and participate equally with men in most tasks. Some head large businesses or hold senior government posts.

The Last Unconquered Land

'If you really want to understand us,' the former Thai prime minister Kukrit Pramoj has advised, 'you must understand water. We are a water people, fluid, but unbreakable.' Water is everywhere: it drenches the hillsides in exuberant vegetation; it flushes the flowers and carries their powerful perfumes into the air; it nurtures the most exotic wild fruits; it floods the rice paddies at each monsoon, fertilises them with rich silt that it brings down from the distant mountains, and provides a habitat for the fish that are the Thais' main source of protein.

Think of a natural amphitheatre as big as France, of high ground surrounding a plain that floods with every heavy rain. This is Thailand and its rice bowl, fed by waters that tumble from the last spurs of the Himalayas, and deluged every May to September by the south-west monsoon. There have been civilisations hereabouts for as long as anywhere on earth, but Thai-speaking people did not begin to make their appearance until comparatively recently. Around the time of King Canute in England, invaders were making their way down the streams and rivers from what is now south and south-west China. The migration intensified when the Mongols of Kublai Khan swept through southern China in the 13th century. And when the settlers spilled onto the plain, remarkable things happened.

River of the King

To understand the Thai way with water, 'you must understand Ayutthaya,' the former prime minister went on. Ayutthaya is an old Sanskrit word meaning 'City of Paradise'. To early European voyagers, it was known as the Venice of the East. The city was easily reached from the sea, yet safe from pirates. Its strategic position on the Chao Phraya – River of the King – was enhanced by diverting another river to turn it into an island. Thirty-seven 'Lords of Life' ruled here over 400 years, conquering neighbours and absorbing chunks of their culture, and creating what was then Siam, and is now Thailand.

Shrines along the Chao Phraya still mark the progress in 1408 of Admiral Cheng Ho, the indefatigable Chinese navigator who had inaugurated trade with Malacca shortly before. Ayutthaya traded elephants and rare woods, golden Buddhas and gem-studded silverware for Chinese porcelain, tea and silks. This brought the Portuguese nosing up river, quickly followed by the Dutch, English, French and many more.

Home is up the ladder. Here, at the bottom, are the laundry and bathing station, waterbus stop, and a choice spot for chatting with neighbours across the klong.

Once the monsoon abates, and the water level recedes, fish are trapped in the klongs *and ponds to provide a plentiful source of protein over the coming months. For all the size of these nets, the fishing is carefully phased to conserve stocks.*

Without its wats *and water, Thai culture would be little different from that of many other parts of South-East Asia. The condition of this dwelling is evidence of the poverty of rural life in less fertile areas. Coconuts provide milk, copra and oil, with their shells used as fuel.*

Seventeenth-century sea captains billowing up to Ayutthaya on the monsoon wind were awed by what they found, for the city gleamed as though made entirely of gold. They counted 1700 *wats* (Buddhist temple-monasteries) with gilded spires reflecting in the *klongs* (canals) that were the water city's thoroughfares, and they wondered over an absence of robbers, 'though the altars be heaped with gold, and the *wats* open day and night'.

What they were marvelling at was Thai Buddhism in action; the founders of the nation had the zest of converts, and practised a particularly pure form, with hopes for a better rebirth pinned to the performance of good deeds and to the adornment and upkeep of ever more splendid *wats.* Almost half the days of the year were devoted to celebrations and festivals, and there was constant music. But there was another side to all this. The society that shaped the Thai character was a strictly stratified pyramid, with power radiating down from a king through a small class of aristocrat-officials, and a benign form of slavery was the lot of many. 'A monarchy, absolute and ostentatious, around which society, in all its forms, is in a state of prostration', was how the British envoy Sir John Bowring described it in the 19th century. 'Every grade is in a state of humble submission to the grade above it, till, culminated in the person and presence of the Sovereign, all the concentrated reverence takes the character of universal adoration...'

Ayutthaya at its height had an estimated 1 million inhabitants, a third of them Chinese, and perhaps 30,000 Persians and Arabs. It had a royal guard of 500 Japanese *samurai,* a stiffening of Portuguese

mercenaries in its armies, and even a Greek foreign minister, until well-founded suspicion of Western intentions led to a period of isolation, although this was less rigorously applied than in Japan.

In April 1767, after a 14-month siege, Ayutthaya was captured and looted by a Burmese army. Its *wats* were destroyed, its gold melted down, and everything of value dragged off as booty, including its royalty, its sacred white elephants, and thousands of craftsmen, musicians, dancers, and even cooks. Thai culture might have been wiped out at a stroke, but remnants rallied to retake the shattered city, and within a dozen years they regained all the lost territory, as well as much of present-day Laos besides.

Ayutthaya was not rebuilt, since the spirits of the place were deemed to be too disturbed already. A new site was chosen downstream, artificially islanded in the same manner as before, with three concentric moats linked together by canals. The first priority was to restore morale, so General Chao Phraya Chakri, who gained the crown (actually, a nine-tiered umbrella), at once set about building temples, the first one enshrining a small, but famously sacred Buddha image. He named the new capital City of Angels, Abode of the Emerald Buddha, but the rest of the world came to know it as Bangkok.

Land of the Free

'It makes you laugh with delight that anything so fantastic could exist on this sombre earth,' Somerset Maugham wrote of Siam in 1925. The celebrated author was then staying at the Oriental Hotel in Bangkok. Joseph Conrad had written *Lord Jim* at the Oriental, and Rudyard Kipling conjured some of his *Just So Stories* there. Siam was definitely the place for storytellers.

Blessed with abundant rice, and with their rivers and *klongs* slippery with fish, the Thais had time to concentrate on what they did best – building beautiful *wats,* and being good Buddhists. Through guile and good luck, their kings had hung onto their independence through a century of rampant European colonisation, and by giving ground at the edges – to the British in the west, and the French in the east and north – they had secured the Thai heartland. The *klong* system had expanded to lattice the flood plain with thousands of miles of waterways bobbing with little boats and floating homes. *Wats* with soaring tiered roofs and eaves lent grandeur to humble villages, and each dawn sent forth lines of saffron-robed monks, the best-

The drift of people into Thailand from beyond the mountains continues to this day. The woman sifting rice in this northern hill village is one of 80,000 Hmong now living in Thailand. The rate of influx quickened dramatically during the Indochina and Vietnam wars.

choreographed army of beggars on earth. Maugham feared that a culture so wondrous and unworldly must surely vanish in the face of rapid modernisation.

The Thai hope had been to take the best of the West, and to reject the rest. Obliged at about the same time as the Japanese to open his country to Western trade, King Mongkut hired an English governess for his 82 children in the 1860s – an event that inspired the musical *The King and I*. He even permitted a road to be built in his capital to please *farang* (Western) residents who wanted to exercise their horses. His son Chulalongkorn hired foreign advisers, toured Europe, and by the turn of the century was ending serfdom and slavery in his own country. Kings now went to Sandhurst and Oxford, and acquired new notions of feminine beauty: women were encouraged to abandon the traditional boyish hair style and pantaloons in favour of longer hair and a modified version of the sarong. But it was reform, not revolution, that the monarchy had in mind, and royal rule was further entrenched through the appointment of princes as ministers and provincial governors. By 1925, Siam had the basic infrastructure of a modern state and a foreign-educated elite who were becoming increasingly fidgety over feudal restriction.

Most Thais will insist today that Somerset Maugham need not have worried about these developments. Seven years after his stay, a group of army officers seized control and obliged the king to sign a constitution, under which he 'ceased to rule, but continued to reign'. It has been that way ever since, with a military-dominated elite controlling the nation's destiny, and much of its wealth, and resolving their squabbles through frequent, and usually bloodless, coups. Instead of scrapping the past, the new oligarchy built upon it, binding the Buddhist religious orders (*sangha*) to the state system, and making royalty the focal point of a fervent new nationalism.

Siam was renamed Thailand in 1939. The literal translation is Land of the Free, and Thais take pride in the fact that they alone in Asia were never colonised or occupied by a European power. His Majesty Bhumibol Adulyadej, Rama IX, is in direct line of descent from one of the generals who led the nation from ruination at

Far from a mere tourist attraction, the floating market is a practical necessity around Thailand's swampy central plain, where a network of canals substitutes for roads. Each sampan is its own small shop, filled with produce paddled in from the farms at daybreak.

Ayutthaya to rebirth in Bangkok, and he and Queen Sirikit are the most revered of all royal couples. There are three 'don'ts' in Thailand. Never point a foot at someone: it's deeply insulting. Never pat a person on the head; to Thais, the head is sacred. And never, never speak lightly of the monarch. Even in private few Thais would dream of criticising the monarchy, and for those that do, there is a strictly enforced *lèse-majesté* law.

Saffron robes and spirit

There were 10 million Thais in Maugham's day, and 15 to 16 million by the end of the Second World War. Now the population is 56 million, and though more than 6 million live in Bangkok, it is the country's only big city.

As far as the eye can see, the flood plain is sliced into tiny geometric pieces glinting in the sun, with

The pagoda-shaped straw hat provides much-needed protection when the sun blazes down on the homeward-bound paddlers.

The klong *becomes clogged with bobbing craft during the early morning market. There is plenty of pushing and shoving, but the farmers' wives are deft waterwomen and nobody takes a ducking.*

The indigo-dyed, long-sleeved cotton shirt (seua maw hawm) *is seen all over rural Thailand and has lately become fashionable with some city intellectuals.*

settlements looking like so many islands in the rainy season, and like palm-fringed oases in the dry. Many of the settlements are a consequence of the population explosion; as a community outgrew its capacity to feed itself, groups would hive off to carve fresh patches out of the jungle, and to repeat the cycle.

No new village is complete without its *wat.* This may be no more than a one-monk cell to start with, but it often gradually expands into an ever-more elaborate complex incorporating *bot* (chapel), dormitory, school, library and community centre. The Buddhist religion has been described as a total way of being. As believers in reincarnation, the Thais seek to gain merit (*bun*) for a later life through acts of *metta* (loving kindness). At dawn each day, 300,000 monks set out from the country's 30,000 *wats* with bowls, offering the faithful the opportunity to gain merit by providing food. Clasped hands touch forehead in an act of humility at their approach, and the monks return to the *wats* to share what has been given. Donating to the temples or, better still, building new ones gains more merit.

The Thai monk is bound by 227 rules of conduct that range from never harming another creature to vows of poverty, celibacy, and abstinence from alcohol. Every Thai male is expected to take the robe and bowl at some time in his life, if only briefly. The military and civil service give men time off with pay for temple sojourns, when they can strive for a perfection hardly possible in their working lives; so do many business companies. Priest, teacher, arbitrator, herbal doctor, psychiatrist, astrologer, exorcist ... the monk is called upon to fill many roles, especially since Buddhism in Thailand happily accommodates folk beliefs of much more ancient origin.

Almost 1000 species of orchid are native to Thailand, and local enthusiasts create ever more hybrids. The most flamboyant wild varieties are found in the northern hills.

Phra phum – earth spirits – lurk everywhere, and have to be constantly appeased. Before any construction venture, auspicious times and sites are determined by temple experts and, even in the most sophisticated reaches of Bangkok, there is hardly a house, block of flats, bank, supermarket or hotel that does not have its spirit house for the resident *phra phum*. Woe betide everyone if the *phra phum* considers itself slighted. As a result, the spirit house is made as attractive as possible, so that it often looks like a kind of dovecote or doll's house perched on a pedestal. It is placed in the choicest, sunniest location, and whenever the main house is improved or refurbished, so, needless to say, is the spirit house.

For further reassurance, Thais arm themselves with amulets and magic charms (*phra kruang)* which they wear around the neck as protection against every imaginable mishap or disaster; most are images of the Buddha, of famously holy monks, or of Indian deities with specialist talents. A powerful talisman can fetch a hefty price, and a shrine that acquires a reputation for producing results becomes a magnet for purposeful

The fragrant ropes of jasmine blossoms on sale in this Bangkok flower market are favourite temple offerings.

The city streets are filled with tempting aromas from pushcart braziers. Thai food is famous for its variety and enticing flavours.

pilgrimage. *Wat Pathumawanaram*, the Lotus Temple, must have particularly sporting spirits, for that is where Bangkok's taxi drivers go to protect their vehicles against accident. *Lak Muang*, a phallic pillar that is the city's foundation stone, is lost beneath millions of tiny squares of gold leaf, pressed layer upon layer by generations of supplicants; it is the object of greatest devotion on days before the drawing of the national lottery. In such a place, so much gold leaf may be pressed into place that a chaff of excess gold drifts about the floor of the shrine.

The iron buffalo

Despite the spectacular example set by kings of the past, Thais are monogamous (except for the Muslim minority near the Malaysian border, and the hill tribes in the far north). Children share equally in the land left by their parents but, with more than two-thirds of the population under the age of 30, sub-divided portions are becoming too small for subsistence, and virgin land is fast running out. This has coincided with an extraordinary surge in the country's economic development, and the intrusion of outside values on a grand scale. Improved communications and government development programmes have loosened age-old loyalties to the village headman (*phu yai baan*) and to the temple. This has created unimagined opportunities, but it has also caused grievous social dislocation where local officials and opportunists of all kinds – traders, contractors, moneylenders and landlords – have taken advantage of their meeker neighbours' ingrained deference to authority.

The benefits and strains are most evident in areas such as the neglected Korat Plateau of the north-east, where soils are poorest, and where no king ever ventured until 1955. It is only relatively recently that electricity has become widely available, and with it the loudspeakers of the national radio, bursting forth with a mix of music, news and advertising. The villagers like it, for it is modern. Television, too, has opened a Pandora's box. Most of all people want a refrigerator, placed in the living area for everyone to admire, or an electric rice cooker. Then they want little tractors, which are known as iron buffaloes, to replace the ubiquitous beast. Temptation leads to debt, often hastened by a Thai weakness for gambling, which leads to borrowing at rates of 20 per cent per month from usurers, unscrupulous government officials or from whoever else cannot wait until the next bad harvest to claim the land at a derisory price. In a sample village in

Called a samlor *in Thailand, the trishaw, or pedicab, is found throughout Asia. These 'drivers' do not own their rickety machines, but must rent them by the day, and on bad days struggle to break even. The advent of the tuk-tuk (motorised samlor) and motorcycle taxi may spell their doom.*

the north-east, it was found that only 60 per cent still owned their own land.

One escape is to seek work elsewhere, often in the Middle East or Singapore, and there is a type of home that has become known as a 'Saudi house'; it is traditional to the extent that it is built on stilts, but it has two storeys, one of brick, with glazed windows and curtains. Below, among the chickens, you may even find a motorbike or two. But for most, any hopes of making enough to build that dream house lie in one direction – Bangkok.

Crazed Bangkok

On approach from the airport, Bangkok has all the appearance of a major catastrophe. A mushroom cloud of smog hangs over endless miles of stalled traffic, around and over which the rush-hour crowds surge in all directions, as if caught in a panicky evacuation. To this beep-and-creep must be added a humidity of almost 90 per cent, temperatures of 35°C, and the aromas of a river that receives 1.6 million cubic yards of raw sewage every day.

Nimble fingers and infinite patience are required to transform the silkworm cocoon into thread, and only then can the weaving begin. Tiny defects in the thread give Thai silk its special appeal.

This woman's solution to survival on the Bangkok streets is a cooking-pot snack bar that she can later hoist on to one end of a springy bamboo pole, balanced by the rest of her meagre possessions on the other.

The *klongs* and elephant paths of old Bangkok were covered over, haphazardly, in an uncontrolled building boom that began in the late 1950s and never stopped. Eighty per cent of Thailand's vehicles are now crammed onto these streets, jammed in what frustrated drivers must regard as permanent gridlock; little three-wheeled 'tuk-tuk taxis', their buzz-saw engines coughing plumes of exhaust, seem to defy gravity as they jump from one stalled lane to the next. The cracked concrete roadway appears to have weathered an earthquake, which in a way it has, for Bangkok is not stable, but heaves and pitches in a light swell. The water table is only a few feet beneath the surface; an effective sewage system is too much to expect and, at the slightest shower, the city floods. At the blink of an eye, sandbags are slapped across doorways, pedestrians grab their shoes in their hands and roll up their trousers, and the battered buses become islands of refuge for the marooned.

The city's population is officially put at 5.8 million, but is generally reckoned to be nearer 8 million, the overflow squeezing a living on streets where it is possible to purchase virtually everything – legal or otherwise – that the heart can desire. The crush of hawkers is greatest on *Charoen Krung*, the New Road of King Mongkut; and it is here that you will still find most of the *farangs* (Westerners), although mostly in the form of tourists nowadays. It was Mongkut's fate to be reborn as Yul Brynner, whose *King and I* antics fascinated Western audiences just when the dawn of the jet age made it possible for ordinary people to go and see for themselves. Thailand's major export-earner used to be rice. By the late 1980s, it was tourism.

In the 1950s, a large but otherwise unremarkable Buddha figure was accidentally dropped from a crane; its thin plaster shell cracked open to reveal a five-and-a-half-ton image in solid gold. The event might be a metaphor for Bangkok itself. Peel away the urban excrescence, and – hey presto! – there are the Temple of the Dawn, the Temple of the Golden Buddha, the Temple of the Reclining Buddha, the Marble Temple, the Temple of the Great Relic ... and 400 more, crowned gloriously by the Grand Palace and *Wat Phra Kaeo* – Temple of the Emerald Buddha. It is as magical a square mile of gold and glitter as exists anywhere on earth.

The tourist comes to gaze where the Thai comes to pray, but no offence is taken by a society in which the spiritual and the secular blend so naturally. The crenellated Palace compound is the heart of both royal and religious Thailand, with the two fusing in the veneration of the Emerald Buddha. Incense, mingled with the scent of flowers and murmured incantations from the prostrate worshippers, rises to the image, which is placed high on a golden pedestal and bathed in green light. The Buddha is less than 30 inches high; it is not made of emerald, and its precise composition is as uncertain as its origins, but mystery only adds to its powers as one of Thailand's holiest symbols. It is personally attended by the King who, three times a year – at the beginning of each hot, rainy, and 'cool' season – changes its robes himself. (*continued on p.82*)

The festival of the elements is being celebrated here. Thai belief is not limited to Buddhist teaching. Animist beliefs are evident in the many rituals dedicated to natural forces.

Parasols from the city of roses

Chieng-Mai – the City of Roses – was isolated from the rest of Thailand until well into the 20th century, and consequently developed its own self-reliant, and quite distinctive, culture. Even now, despite rapid modernisation, it sustains a rich variety of handicrafts that are not practised elsewhere. Among these, the making of one object in particular has come to symbolise the special charm of Chieng-Mai – the humble paper umbrella, which ranges in size from the minuscule to splendid spans of up to 10 feet.

So many umbrellas are made around nearby Baw Sang that it is better known as the umbrella village. The main road is festooned with bright canopies drying in the sun next to the craft workshops. Despite such mass production, every part is entirely hand-made – even the strong, translucent paper, which is pounded from the bark of a local tree. The shaft is of cane, and the ribwork is an assembly of fine bamboo strips, over which layers of paper are carefully pasted. Artists apply pictures of flowers and birds with a few practised brush-strokes, and then a final protective varnish is applied. Light enough to be the perfect parasol under a torrid sun, and yet able at the same time to resist the hammer-blows of a monsoon storm, a good-quality Chieng-Mai umbrella has practicality as well as charm.

No city has adapted itself more to the instant gratification required by jet travellers. At the top end of the scale, the venerable Oriental has been voted the world's best hotel. Bellhops in Yul Brynner pants and white gloves skip about the marble lobby where a fountain gurgles, and slim, beautiful women wait to serve guests whose Thai experience will be as near to the dream image of the country as money can make it. The Oriental is augmented by a score more five-star hotels, and innumerable of lesser magnitude, more than 11,000 restaurants, hundreds of discos, and an unconscionable number of Bangkok's speciality, the massage parlour.

At first light, stop-over tourists can ride the back canals around the Temple of Dawn, watching the monks paddle from home to home collecting food, then lose themselves among the temples of the inner city. In the afternoon they can shop for sapphires and silks in air-conditioned arcades, before dining in spicy splendour along the river. Finally they plunge into the most lurid nightlife in Asia.

The menu of vices on open offer in Bangkok after dark is mind-boggling, and by means of such innovations as the 'sex tour' it has brought a new

Saffron-robed monks dine on the offerings they have collected on their early morning ramble. Virtually every young Thai male spends a few months as a novice monk; some take the robe for life, renouncing wealth and all worldly pleasures, and striving for a state of perfection through meditation and studying the Buddha's teachings. Buddhists believe that their everyday behaviour will count in future lives and will determine their hopes of eventually entering Nirvana, a state in which the soul is at one with the universe – freed from the toil and suffering of constant rebirth.

Wat Benchamabopitr, *popularly known as the Marble Temple, is the most recent of Bangkok's major temples. Completed in 1910, it featured such innovations as Carrara marble and Western-style stained-glass windows. A* wat *is much more than a place of worship and a monastery: it is the focal point of local life, serving a myriad social functions: school, orphanage, social centre, library, playground, hospital, and even a sanctuary for stray animals.*

Worship is a part of everyday life: a moment taken to visit the temple viharn, *where the Buddha images are kept, and to kneel for an instant in contemplation, holding an incense stick and floral offering in joined hands. Petals are cast towards the image, and the incense stick joins hundreds of others in the big copper jar. Buddhism does not exclude belief in other faiths, but Christian missionaries have struggled since the early 19th century to win converts, with little success.*

Thailand's hill tribes form a constantly shifting mosaic across the rugged northern hills. They have no set territories, though some have a preference for a particular altitude. Their rickety bamboo homes are designed for easy disassembly and transportation, since villages move every few years when the soil is exhausted.

Each tribe has its own traditions and beliefs, its own language, and its own style of dress. This woman is a Lahu, a tribe noted for its hunting skills and complex religion in which 'blessing' is sought through rites and incantations.

dimension to the concept of the package holiday. Thais have a pragmatic attitude towards prostitution and gained a great deal of experience and custom from the R & R (rest and recreation) frontline of American forces in the Vietnam War. The labour force is recruited largely from poor rural areas. Most of the prostitutes are under 18, and 10 per cent are 12 or less; indeed, some have been sold into virtual slavery by their parents.

Even hardened travel writers are sometimes taken aback by the lengths to which the Thais have gone in packaging their charms and wonders: 'the theme-park kingdom', as Margo Kaufmann of the *Los Angeles Times* once called it. The transformation is nowhere more complete than at Pattaya, which little more than two decades ago was a quiet fishing village on golden sands. A new road constructed in the 1970s brought it within 90 minutes of Bangkok, and soon it was being touted

as the 'Thai Riviera'. By the end of the 1980s, Pattaya had become a neon blur of bars and hotels proffering every manner of commercial sex and suffering from the inevitable pollution, water shortages, and other effects of excess. 'Truly, the Garden of Earthly Delights in the most Boschean sense,' is how one guidebook put it, in a reference to the nightmarish paintings of Hieronymus Bosch.

Imaginative enterprises include the packaging of the infamous Death Railway and its Bridge on the River Kwai. The railway, and the graves of thousands of Allied prisoners who died constructing it for the Japanese, lay largely forgotten in lush green hills 80 miles north of Bangkok, until the Tourism Authority recognised its potential. Now there are floating restaurants and raft trips on the Kwai, and for a week in December the bridge is 'bombed' nightly as part of a spectacular sound and light show. It is possible to take in the Grand Palace, Death Railway and the Bangkok fleshpots all in a one-day stopover.

Likening tourist Thailand to an oriental Disneyland, critic Margo Kaufmann defined the product as split into 'Beachland', 'Sexland', 'Ruinsland' (Ayutthaya and other archaeological sites), and, in the far north, 'Trekland with its popular attraction, the Golden Triangle – Opiumland'.

Cities and tribes of the north

Elephants shamble on silent, rubbery feet down a jungle path to the river, with only the faint clinking of their polished chains and the hollow ring of their teakwood bells signalling their approach. There is dust, woodsmoke and birdsong in the air above Chieng-Mai, the northern capital. Higher still are the hill tribes and the little, lost valleys where the poppies grow.

Before a railway was blasted through the hills, river and elephant were the only ways of reaching the north, and even today the people of Bangkok still regard the northern part of the country as strangely exotic. The region remained a semi-autonomous principality until the 1930s. When King Prajadhipok entered the city of Chieng-Mai at the head of a stately procession of elephants it was the first visit by a reigning monarch for 150 years.

Lisu women wear distinctive red-and-turquoise dresses. Proud and competitive, the 20,000 Lisu have prospered more than some other groups, because they are major opium cultivators.

Picturesque costumes obscure the harsh realities of hilltop life – such as having to haul water from the valley floor. The Akha woman depicted here is able to carry about 9 gallons in hollow bamboos packed into a pannier; this is then harnessed to a yoke which is supported by a leather strap around the forehead.

A common characteristic of the hill tribes is their love of silver jewellery – often in the form of old Indian silver rupees from the days of the Raj. Among the Akha, the practice is so extreme that they even work in the fields loaded down by heavy finery.

These Hmong women tending a poppy patch in the Golden Triangle make a pretty picture from an alarming scene. This region is the source of at least half the world's illicit opium. Straddling the borders of Thailand, Burma, and Laos, it is impossible to police effectively. The denuded hill-side beyond points to another of Thailand's problems.

In fact, Chieng-Mai can claim greater antiquity than Bangkok or even its predecessor Ayutthaya. It was originally founded over 700 years ago and in 1296 became the capital of the kingdom of Lanna Thai, a group of northern tribes forged into a single nation under King Mangrai. The new kingdom expanded and continued to thrive until the 15th century, after which it was conquered first by Ayutthaya, and then by Burma. Only in 1775 did it return to the Thai fold, and even then remained a semi-autonomous princedom ruled by its own dynasty of princes until 1938.

Today, Chieng-Mai is famous for the beauty of its girls, for its crafts, and its intricately carved teakwood temples, which are filled with statues of fantastic mythical beasts and friendly monks. Even the rhythms of the northern dialect are slower and more relaxed; but

here again, life is changing fast. The once-remote city set about its lotus-filled moat has sprouted huge hotels, high-rise apartment blocks, and factories; ferroconcrete has vanquished teak, and the rasp of tuk-tuks now drowns the gentle tapping of the silversmiths. Tourism has had a major impact, and there is liable to be a currency exchange van parked at the end of that elephant path.

Snagged in the craggy hills and mountains that spread out between Chieng-Mai and the borders with Burma and Laos are more than half a million Tibeto-Burman people belonging to as many as 20 different hill tribes – nobody is quite sure how many there are. Semi-nomadic, with scant regard for national frontiers, they range from substantial quasi-national groups such as the Karen, Hmong, Lahu and Akha, to wispy fragments such as the Phi Thong Luang (Spirits of the Yellow Leaves) who were discovered only recently. Most have lived in Thailand for a relatively short time, having arrived as refugees from one of the many regional conflicts. One group, however, the Lawa, can claim to be among the country's original inhabitants – they first settled there as early as the 8th century AD.

Unlike the people in the rest of Thailand, the tribespeople still mostly wear their traditional costumes, which introduce attractive splashes of black, white, red and blue to the streets of Chieng-Mai when they come down for special festivals. Their customs, meanwhile, are as varied as their dress, but most share the disconcerting habit of cultivating the opium poppy, which they do by a destructive type of slash-and-burn forest agriculture.

The poppy resin is extracted using a scraper: some to fill tribal opium pipes; some to be refined into heroin and to ooze into the veins of addicts around the world by a thousand secret routes.

The little oily ball is carefully placed on a skewer, then put to a flame next to the small aperture of the opium pipe. A little sputter; a pungent smell; a long puff and then another. Four, ten, twenty pipes later, time and dimension lose their meaning.

The golden triangle

The point at which Thailand, Burma and Laos meet forms the heart of the Golden Triangle, which is named after the fortunes made by shadowy warlords in the years since the Second World War, when this region became the major source of the world's illicit opium and heroin.

The poppy grows well on the misty mountain slopes, but was not the cause of any major problems until the upheavals of the Indochina and Vietnam wars rent apart a region that had once been described by a British official as 'an Asian Arcady'. Decades of warfare dislodged whole societies, and many opium-growing tribespeople slipped over the Thai borders, where they became pawns in a sinister game contested by a bewildering variety of guerrilla forces, including offshoots of the Kuomintang Army of Chiang Kai Shek which fled China after the Communist victory in 1949 and had been in Thailand since 1961. Some of these groups became conduits for crime syndicates operating mainly through Thailand.

Urged on by the United States Government, Thai army rangers and helicopter-borne border police make periodic sweeps to destroy poppy fields and secret heroin refineries but, until recently, too many government officials had become corrupted for this to have much impact. The action was hottest along a high ridge on the Burmese border, where the warlord Khun Sa's stronghold was located only a few miles from some of his Kuomintang rivals. In the late 1980s, Thai forces attacked in strength and drove Khun Sa across the border. The Kuomintang town of Mae Salong was renamed Sankatiri (Peacetown), and the area was treated to systematic 'pacification': roads improved, Thai language and culture promoted, and substitute crops, such as tea and coffee, strawberries, even Brussels sprouts, encouraged.

A new kind of army has taken to the hills. By motorbike, truck, and slogging on foot, tourists come to peer at the hill tribes, to raft down the tumbling streams, to sniff expectantly for the forbidden opium. The hills, meanwhile, still echo occasionally to the crack of unexplained gunfire, and routes get suddenly closed for no very clear reason.

But nothing seems to stand in the way of Thai 'development'. What had been the Thai Communist Party's mountain hideaway until 1982 has been proclaimed a national park and museum, and scores of companies offer 'hill-tribe treks' into the high Triangle. Package tours make a beeline for Ban Sob Ruak, a village on the junction of the Kok and Mekong rivers, which is the point at which Thailand, Burma, and Laos meet. What with its restaurants, its souvenir stands, a Poppy Guest House and a Golden Triangle Resort, the Triangle is fast becoming another of Thailand's tourist traps.

The extraordinarily supple grace of the Thai dancer is attained through years of rigorous training, which must start at an early age for the body to acquire the necessary elasticity. For example, a young girl's fingers will be 'manipulated' by her mother to make them supple enough to be able to bend backwards so as almost to touch the wrist. Classical khon and lakhon dances interpret the great Hindu legends through a series of highly stylised gestures and were once performed only for royalty. At certain shrines, lakhon troupes may be hired for performances that are holy offerings in themselves.

Malaysia

The Malay peninsula projects like some ancient sword from Asia's south-eastern corner. Jungle-clad mountains form its near-impenetrable central spine, with lush hills and plateaus spreading out on either side. Across the South China Sea, meanwhile, is Malaysia's other half: Sabah and Sarawak on northern Borneo. Diversity of landscapes is matched by a diversity of peoples – native Malays, Chinese, Indians, not to mention little-known jungle tribes. But none of this has stopped Malaysia's economic success. It is the world's largest producer of rubber, palm oil and tin, and is an important exporter of hardwoods, gas and oil.

***Previous page:** Life could hardly be simpler on remote stretches of the Malay peninsula's east coast. Boats leave with the tide and drift back slowly, dragging their nets. Fish are abundant, but once the monsoon blows, fishermen will not venture forth for three months.*

A Dayak blowpipe loaded with a tiny pellet can bring down a bird perched more than 100 feet up in the forest canopy. Even so, most of the hunters of Borneo have abandoned their traditional weapon for the greater firepower of rifle or shotgun.

The giant argus pheasant is difficult to approach, but its strange, melodious cry is a giveaway. Dayaks covet its magnificent feathers for their headdress.

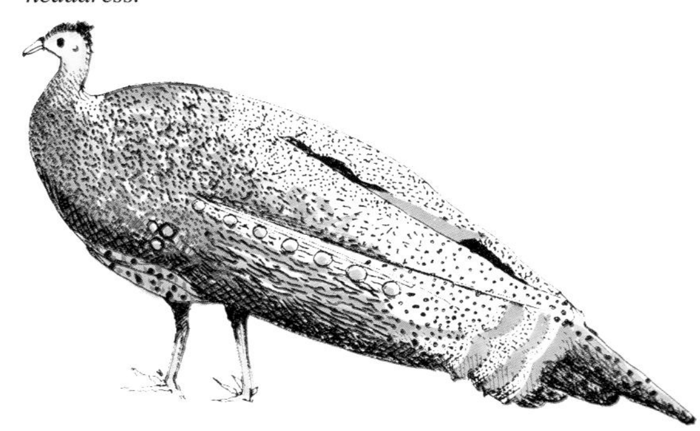

Green Heart of the Orient

The Malay peninsula stretches its verdant, mountainous spine almost as far as the equator. High table lands tip down to beautiful, unbroken coasts on either side. This is West Malaysia. East Malaysia is 500 miles away across the South China Sea and comprises nearly one third of the huge island of Borneo.

A shared geology, as well as political convenience, holds together these two segments of the Malaysian Federation. Both ride the Sunda platform, an ancient block of granite and sedimentary rock that once constituted a South-East Asian sub-continent, but is now half-submerged and seared around the edge by the seismic ring of fire that arches from Indonesia to the Philippines, and all the way up to Japan.

Lords of the jungle

This is one of the rainiest regions on earth and, in its natural state, the land is mantled in jungle from shoreline to mountaintop. These are the oldest of all the world's equatorial rainforests, far older than those of Africa and the Amazon, and they are in consequence the most richly endowed.

For more than 120 million years, the jungle has lain undisturbed. Only its dimensions have changed with the rise and fall of the oceans caused by the cycle of ice ages, and with the gradual erosion of the landmass from aeons of pounding rain and searing sun. As a result, there has been time for nature to run a riot of every conceivable kind of evolutionary experiment. The variety of vegetation is staggering. It has been reasoned that locked away in the Malaysian forest pharmacy – if all of its elusive juices and essences could be isolated and then analysed – there must be cures and therapies for just about every disease known to mankind.

The raw numbers are staggering: at least 10,000 plant species, including 2000 varieties of tree; there are 200 types of palm alone. The jungle menagerie is enough to send Noah back to the drawing board: more than 200 species of mammal, 250 of reptile, some 500 types of exotic bird, and at least 150,000 varieties of insect. Tigers and leopards still stalk its glades; there are elephants and, still, a few rhinos, tapirs and bears; a multitude of monkeys; 100 species of snakes, including cobras, vipers and pythons; and all manner of fantastic creatures, such as the tiny mouse deer, the flying squirrel, lizards, and even frogs, whose bodies have become specially adapted for gliding about the forest canopy. There are even snakes which can fling themselves about from branch to branch, like some kind of rather alarming trapeze artist. This is the same jungle that held the pioneer British evolution theorist Alfred Russel Wallace happily captive and 'trembling with excitement' for several years towards the end of the 19th century.

In its natural state, full 'triple canopy' rainforest clogs all the lowland and valleys, and mantles the mountainsides for up to 4000-5000 feet. Colossal

This Dayak longhouse, typical of many scattered along the rivers of East Malaysia (Borneo), has much to recommend it as a multi-family hamlet under one roof. The Malaysian Government would rather the Dayaks moved into conventional villages, but the people are hard to persuade.

The lotus plant is many things to the people of South-East Asia. As a popular design motif it is seen as a symbol for wisdom, grace and harmony, but it also has more practical uses: its fleshy roots can be eaten; its seeds are a nutty delicacy; and its leaves are useful as cattle fodder.

200 foot trees soar towards the distant light, through layers of lesser growths: strangling fig and tentacled liana, swinging vine and clinging orchid, blood-sucking leech and carnivorous pitcher plant. Above 5000 feet, this gradually gives way to forests of evergreen oak, chestnut and fern. Higher still, the mountains crest in a surreal, sodden landscape dominated by gnarled dwarf trees, trailing tendrils of cloud vapour and dripping with lichen, hanging mosses and the occasional gorgeous orchid.

From the evidence of a skull discovered in the Niah Caves of Sarawak, we know that bands of humans began to infiltrate the jungle at least 40,000 years ago. These bands had the forest to themselves, hunting, gathering fruits and living in harmony with nature for perhaps 35,000 years, before they were pushed aside by a more advanced people who seem to have spread down from present-day southern China to occupy the peninsula and the islands beyond. These so-called Proto-Malays began to clear patches of jungle for cultivation, and were lords of the forest for perhaps 2000 years before they, in turn, were pushed aside by newcomers who had learned how to work metal but who were of much the same stock, although with some added infusions of Chinese, Indian and Arab blood. The new wave made their presence felt from around 300 BC onwards, and their direct descendants are the Malays of today.

Word of the 'golden peninsula' reached Ancient Rome, conveyed through Indian traders who had begun to make great voyages to China, and had found they could take on spices, gold and aromatic sandalwood on the way. The narrow strait between Sumatra and the peninsula became infested with pirates, with the result that some of the traders established settlements along the Malay rivers and hauled their goods overland to dodge the menace.

Trading kingdoms that were influenced by a large influx of merchants and priests from India rose and fell, until in 1403 a Sumatran prince hit upon the perfect combination when he founded the port of Melaka (Malacca) at what was both the narrowest part of the strait and the point where the monsoon winds met.

The longhouse is flanked by a large open terrace, or tanju, *that has many uses. This one serves as a chicken run and drying yard for clothes and fishing gear. In regions reached by tourists, the* tanju *serves as a dance platform.*

Malacca gained the protection of China's Ming emperors, and so dominated trade from every direction that it became extremely rich and powerful. It was through Malacca that the Islamic faith spread around the whole region so quickly. After a century, the Portuguese captured the port, forcing the sultan to flee on his fighting elephant, and they and the Dutch held it in turn for almost 300 years.

Then came the British, who made Malacca one of their Straits Settlements, and over the course of the 19th century – bit by bit and sultanate by sultanate – they gained effective control of all the territory that would one day become Malaysia. The jungle, meanwhile, which until now had hardly been touched, suffered slash wounds from mid-century onwards, as tin miners tore at its heart and rubber planters peeled it strip by strip.

In these hot and humid conditions, peninsular Malaysia becomes a shimmering prism of green, olive, almond, emerald, malachite, chartreuse and aquamarine – reflected off the patchwork of rice paddies and coconut groves, rubber and palm oil estates, mangroves and primal jungle. Suddenly, lead-black clouds roll over, and it rains and rains. Torrents cascade down the mountainsides and, with the power of a fire hose, they flush away the top-soil left exposed by the careless cultivator, miner or logger.

As in most of the tropics, the lushness of the jungle hides a desperately fragile ecology. The soil is poor and, once the forest is cleared, it is washed out or leeched into useless aridity within a couple of monsoons. The rivers run red-brown mud, their precious cargo silting estuaries, or building up the mangrove swamps. Malacca provides a yard-stick: in the time since the Portuguese ruled, the silt from the Malacca River has pushed back the sea to well beyond cannonball range of the old fort. The erosion process is age-old, but the activities of mankind quicken it immeasurably.

Land of the White Rajah

What happened to the peninsula over centuries has been happening to East Malaysia in a few decades. Well within living memory, this was one of the most mysterious places on earth. For primitive savagery, the 'wild men' of Borneo were seen to be in a class of their own, and no boys' adventure magazine was complete without a lurid encounter with one of these headhunting horrors.

Even the tallest tales had a grounding in extraordinary fact. There was, for instance, a White Rajah reigning over 50,000 square miles of jungle and swamp. It was in Sarawak, given in 1841 by the Sultan of Brunei to a dashing young Englishman named James Brooke; as a reward for his services in sorting out the tribal warfare that was then raging. Brooke used his schooner, the *Royalist*, to put down piracy, and his charisma to win the trust of warring Malay and Dayak tribesmen. His descendants continued to rule Sarawak as benign despots for more than a century, during which time neighbouring North Borneo, which was still under the control of the sultans of Brunei, also came under British 'protection'.

The sultans of Brunei were wiser than they knew. Oil was discovered under the small coastal enclave that they retained, and which they still rule today as the last absolute monarchs in Asia – and with a seat in the United Nations! The balance of what had been theirs became East Malaysia: Sarawak and Sabah (as North Borneo was renamed). The terrain still has the outward appearance of an unconquered jungle fortress, soaring in Sabah to the 13,500-foot summit of Mount Kinabalu, which is the highest peak in the whole of South-East Asia. Towns cling to the coastline; scattered settlements cling to the rivers.

Up-river are the Dayaks, a name applied to a number of tribes with different languages and customs. Many have converted to Christianity, but old ways persist.

Young longhouse dwellers clamber aboard in the traditional way. Like a medieval drawbridge, the notched tree trunk can be raised at night to thwart intruders. The 10ft gap under the longhouse protects it from seasonal river flooding and provides night-time shelter for chickens, ducks, goats and pigs which the non-Muslim Dayaks raise in quantity.

Mats are laid out at the entrance to each home along the ruai *(corridor) of the longhouse, which provides a refuge from the heat of the day and the torrential downpours of the monsoon. In the evening, lit by an electric generator, the* ruai *takes on the life of a village street.*

Tattoos are worn by both sexes as ritual protection and decoration, and charms and omens – often the cry of a particular bird – are important. So are earlobes; the longer the lovelier. After years of wearing weighted plugs, some Dayak women's earlobes dangle right down to their chests. Dayaks are also famous for their longhouses.

A longhouse is built on stilts, about 10 feet off the ground. It is a village, or more precisely a street, under one roof, and often accommodates 50 or more families, each with its own *bilik*, or private quarters, with a door on to a spacious bamboo-floored corridor (*ruai*) that runs the length of the building. The *ruai* is the focus of community activity. Beyond is an outer verandah (*tanju*) which is used as a drying yard for clothes, rice and pepper, and for collecting rainwater, nowadays usually in old petrol cans. There is also a loft for storing grain. In the old days, this is where a Dayak chief hid his daughter until some warrior proved himself heroic enough to claim her as his bride – usually by taking a head or two.

Dayaks like to point out that rules of chivalry were observed in headhunting, and that women and children were invariably spared. Head-counts were tattooed on the knuckles, and it is with pride that those still able to do so display their score. Though headhunting is now banned, trophies are not, and smoke-blackened skulls of Japanese soldiers from the Second World War, and others that have been taken in the course of more recent conflicts with Indonesia and Communist insurgents, still dangle from longhouse beams alongside various earlier acquisitions.

The Iban are the main Dayak group. Proud, democratic and immensely hospitable despite what has sometimes happened in the past, they have adapted the longhouse life to changing conditions: self-sufficient in rice and other basic foods, they produce some rubber, cocoa and sago as cash crops for sale down-river, along with basketware and other handicrafts. Many longhouses now have an electric generator to power refrigerator, TV and lights. The rifle or shotgun has replaced the blowpipe, and canoes have outboard motors. How long the lifestyle can be sustained in the face of steady desertion by the young to the outside world is debatable. But there is a more immediate threat to the forest dwellers, particularly those known as the *orang ulu*, the interior people, nomadic bands of hunter-gatherers who rely totally upon the jungle's bounty.

The major product of the forest used to be the edible nests of the cave swift, used for Chinese soup. Nowadays, it is the forest itself. Through the 1980s, Malaysia stepped up its forestry until it accounted for two-thirds of the world export of tropical wood; 40 per cent of this came from Sarawak, where an estimated 1000 square miles of forest was being logged annually for its teak and other precious hardwoods. Less valuable softwoods are usually left alone, but the damage is severe, and regeneration uncertain.

As the jungle chorus of bird and beast became drowned by the roar of tractors and chain saws, a chorus of protest was taken up by the Western governments and international bodies concerned by the dangers posed by wholesale destruction of the world's rainforests. But when Dayaks set up jungle barricades to stop the loggers, many were arrested, and the pace of logging was intensified. Most immediately threatened of all tribes were the Punan, who are thought to be directly descended from the oldest Malaysian of them all – the Niah cave man.

In addition to rice, Malays cultivate green vegetables with which to garnish their meat and fish curries. Vegetarian dishes are also popular, and delicious.

Tops, kites and birdsong

Slight but robust, shy but opinionated, the Malays differ from the tribes of Borneo, and from the tribal remnants of Orang Asli ('Original People') who are scattered through the jungle of the peninsula; they are distinguished by their Islamic faith and by their settled attachment to a particular plot of land. The Malays are born farmers. Urban life is too hurried and too impure for their comfort, and those who settle in the city do so only because their work requires that they must.

The Malay world revolves around the kampongs, pleasant villages on stilts, along the roads or scattered among the rice paddies and coconut groves. The elevated houses of weathered wood, with verandahs and unglazed windows, look as welcoming as the narrow footpaths that thread between red hibiscus (the national flower) and giant lilium bushes, and under fruit trees bearing papaya, rambutan, mangosteen and banana. A neat, flower-decked courtyard circles each house. The washing flaps in the breeze; fish are drying on mats, and there are baskets of vegetables and pimento. There are also goats, ducks and chickens, but definitely no pigs, for that is where the Muslim Malays part company with the Dayak and Chinese, who both love pork. The courtyards are swept constantly, and each has a basin where people wash their feet before climbing the steps. Cleanliness is a virtue taught by the Koran, and the

Malays take it very much to heart; shoes are always left outside to keep the home clean.

The interior is modest, comprising two or three rooms, which are sometimes separated by a colourful curtain; they are simply furnished with chests and wicker baskets, mattresses or mats for sleeping, and sometimes with mosquito nets that are rolled up during the day. On the walls are photographs of weddings, parents, children and a large framed portrait of the ruling sultan. The small kitchen area has a pantry where rice, dried fish, oil and prepared curries are kept. Being on stilts helps to keep the home cool and dry.

Kampong life, in turn, revolves around the rice cycle. Rice was introduced to Malaysia from India about 2000 years ago. As the country's staple food, it is respected, even revered; for example, ripe ears are hung in the home to ensure prosperity and happiness. The task of cultivating it is shared out according to a strict pattern between the sexes: the men till the neat, muddy paddies with their buffalo; they do the sowing and manage the harvest, but the women come to help transplant the seedlings, and tie and gather the sheaves at harvest time; in their big, bobbing conical hats, they fill the paddy with cheerful chatter.

A Hindu priest meditates under a papaya tree at the entrance to a holy grotto. Malaysia's numerous large limestone caverns are in great demand as Hindu sanctuaries. Best-known are the Batu Caves near Kuala Lumpur, where tens of thousands gather for the Thaipusam festival.

Eight porters are only just enough to transport this giant python, which is over 30 feet long, to market. It will not become a hunting trophy; instead, it will be sliced up and sold by the chunk as a delicacy. The Chinese are fond of python meat, as they are of boa constrictors and baby crocodiles, but python is said to be the most savoury.

The Government wants Malaysia to become self-sufficient in rice, and new hybrid brands have been introduced which can yield two harvests a year. This accelerated activity is regretted by some, since it doubles the work, but there are advantages. Incomes are up, allowing the young to own motorbikes and electric guitars, and to dream of becoming pop stars or even entering a profession. Two harvests a year also provide two excuses for a party.

A kampong harvest festival is unlike any other, for where else do kite-flying and top-spinning contests top the bill? The Malay *gasing* (top) is no child's toy. It is about the size of a dinner plate, can weigh 13 to 15 pounds, and has the roar of a cannon firing when 'thrown' on its tightly-wound, 15-foot cord. Some tops are carefully machine-tooled, with precious metal inlays; others are quite crudely carved. There are scything battles between teams of fighting tops, and

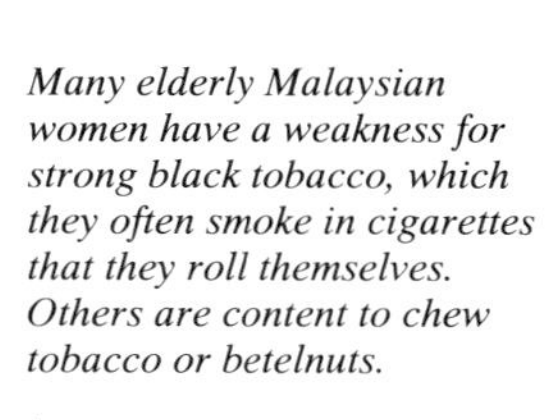

Many elderly Malaysian women have a weakness for strong black tobacco, which they often smoke in cigarettes that they roll themselves. Others are content to chew tobacco or betelnuts.

The Malay spinning top is no child's toy. It is heavy – weighing up to 15 lbs – and is let go with such pent-up energy that a spinning time of one hour is normal. Much of the secret lies in the way the spindle-cord is wound and then released, and there are many strategies to prolong momentum.

there are also endurance contests. The tops spin, and spin, and spin ... only after an hour does the atmosphere become electric, and the shouting, whistling and cheering of rival fans mount. The all-time record spin is close to two hours, but whatever his personal best, a local champion is the idol of his village. Health is, however, a consideration in all this – boys under the age of 16 are discouraged from participating, because of the danger of shoulder strain or dislocation.

Most Malaysian kites are shaped like butterfly wings, and are works of art in themselves. When trying for the longest and highest flight, each village launches as many kites as it can, some with attachments that hum or whistle a strange music in the wind. The critical moment is at the moment of launching, and a really competitive kite is so heavy and so broad that this manoeuvre often requires three men. Dancing in the blue sky, these colourful kites are the epitome of the kampong spirit.

Birdsong is another symbol of kampong life – and another, rather unlikely source of competition although, in this case, the need for patience and silence limits the crowds to the discerning few. After long periods of conditioning, the birds are placed in cages on top of 30ft poles, where, unconcerned by the tension below, they respond at full trill to the encouragement of their masters.

their hands. They catch it with their heels, toes, head, shoulders, chest and thighs, before bouncing it high, taking it again and rolling it. Then, with a crafty flick, they send it soaring once more, as the crowd gasps its knowledgeable appreciation ...

A kampong party night is a lively, intimate confection of lamp-lit laughter, dancing and theatricals. The *berdikir barat* is another inter-village tussle, this time played around the bonfire by teams of quick-witted conversationalists, who thrust and parry with facetious statements and funny or deriding retorts. It helps to create a mood of good humour for performances of *makyong* or *menora* – traditional forms of Malaysian song-and-dance drama which are accompanied by an orchestra of gongs, wind and string instruments. *Makyong* is performed exclusively by women, with the principal role (the *makyong*) narrating and directing the action. In *menora*, men play even the female roles in adaptations from the *Ramayana*, the Indian epic.

But the most popular way to enjoy the stories of the *Ramayana* is in the shadow play of the famous Wayang puppets, as performed by the *To' Dalang*, the puppet master who gives life and voice to Prince Rama, his beautiful wife Sita, his brother Lakshmana, the monkey-god Hanuman, the evil Ravana, the happy jokers Pa'Dogah and Wak Long, and scores of other

The wau bulan, *or moon kite, was chosen as the symbol of Malaysia's national airline; the name comes from the crescent-shaped tailpiece. Some kites are so large that three people are required to launch them.*

Songbird contests are a feature of Malaysian life, and champion birds can cost thousands of pounds. For the less affluent, a simple turtle dove provides as much pleasure.

The kampong has its own martial art: *silat,* an ancient Malay form of self-defence which is similar to Japanese karate. *Silat* was once a deadly art. Now it is more of a mime play by young men dressed in black, their combat a series of swift, studied moves, which slow down at moments of special subtlety for the crowd to appreciate.

Dexterity, balance and concentration are also required in *sepak raga,* surely the most basic of all national sports. *Sepak raga* is a contest in ball-control: a kind of one-man soccer without teams or goalposts. Spectators form a circle round the players, who flick a wicker ball into the air with their feet, then keep it aloft for as long as possible without ever touching it with

These sea turtle eggs are destined for human consumption but, in exchange, the turtles have been given a helping hand. Beach guards collect tens of thousands of eggs to incubate and release into the sea as baby turtles, before attending to the requirements of the eating public. The Malaysian Chinese are very fond of turtle eggs, believing them to be an aphrodisiac.

characters. This is a night-long entertainment, and it is dawn before the villains have been duly punished, the good have been suitably rewarded, and Prince Rama made happy.

The greater the distance from the Malacca Strait, and from the paths of invasion and migration, the more relaxed is kampong life. For a very long time, the east coast was isolated from the west by mountain and jungle, and so this is where Malay culture is still at its purest. Even here, however, modern life is beginning to make itself felt: the mountains are now pierced by motorways, and tourists have discovered its beaches and coral islands – as have the oil prospectors!

It was here, on the island of Tioman (renamed Bali-Hai for the occasion), that Hollywood filmed *South Pacific*. Elsewhere, fishing villages dot the coast, each with its brightly-painted shoal of boats waiting for the tide to carry them to the fish. In the months in which the north-east monsoon blows, the fishermen wisely stay at home, or choose this moment to make the trip to Mecca.

Here you will find the best craftsmen in silver and copper, the best cloth weavers and batik experts, the best traditional dancers and actors, and the best top-spinners; for Kelantan, the most distant state, on the Thai border, boasts a whole array of Malay superlatives. The beaches around Kota Bharu, the Kelantan capital, have the most romantic names. Pantai Irama is the Beach of Melody; there is a Beach of the Whispering Breeze, and even a Beach of Passionate Love, although Muslim sensibilities ensure that this is not literally so. It was here, 95 minutes before the attack on Pearl Harbor, that Japanese forces came ashore on December 7, 1941, to begin the Second World War in the East.

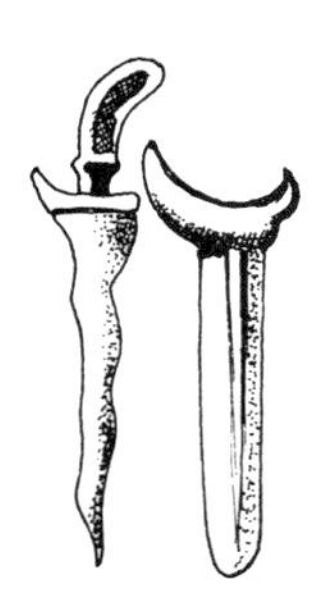

The kris *is a symbol of royal power among Malay peoples. The wavy blade, sheathed in a richly decorated scabbard, is often credited with magical or supernatural powers. The head of a family keeps the* kris *that his father handed down to him in a safe place, so that one day he too can hand it down to one of his sons.*

Tin mine and rubber tree

Over the mountains lies the Malaysia that was moulded by the British. Here, along the western length of the peninsula, are the cities, the plantations and the centres of immigrant populations which, by their numbers and energy, have at times threatened to dispossess the Malays of their own country.

There were Hindu kingdoms on the west coast more than 1000 years ago, and Chinese trading posts proliferated in the wake of the Ming Admiral Cheng Ho's voyages to Malacca in the early 1400s. But large-scale migration from China and India took place only under the British in the late 19th and early 20th centuries. As part of its policy of indirect rule through local sultans, Britain left the kampong culture of their subjects more or less undisturbed, and brought in Chinese labour instead to build the roads and railways, and to mine the tin that was the peninsula's richest prize.

Tin had been mined for centuries in the state of Perak but, with the development of the tin can, demand became insatiable from the 1860s. The result was a tin rush, and an influx of Chinese miners to brawling settlements which eventually grew into cities such as Ipoh and Kuala Lumpur. By the start of the 20th century, Malaya was producing half the world's tin, and very soon after that, it was producing more than half the world's rubber.

The introduction of rubber is a dramatic story. Seeds collected in Brazil by Sir Henry Wickham were germinated at Kew Gardens in London, and a few sent to Malaya as an experiment. British planters had cleared patches of jungle to grow coffee and pepper,

These Iban women in full ceremonial dress prepare to dance for a party of tourists, for a few Malay dollars or a carton of cigarettes. Tourism is a mixed blessing, since it encourages the preservation of tribal arts, but tends at the same time to debase them.

and mocked Henry 'Rubber' Ridley, the botanist who urged them to try the strange tree which took at least seven years to become productive. The invention of the bicycle tyre, then the development of the motor car, converted them to Ridley's enthusiasm for growing rubber.

Row upon regimented row of rubber tree replaced swathes of jungle, to be tapped by gangs of labourers brought across from southern India. Even now, despite a declining call for natural latex, a good 5500 square miles of West Malaysia is under rubber, or well over half the total cultivated area (and one or two of the original seedlings brought from Kew still grow in golden domed Kuala Kangsar, seat of the Sultan of Perak).

Many Indian workers perished from fever and general neglect on the plantations. Some of their descendants still tap rubber or cut oil palms for desperately low wages, but many others have become shopkeepers, teachers, lawyers and doctors. The Chinese were much more numerous – already 2 million by the turn of the century – and much more determined in their pursuit of success. Right from the begining, they filled the new cities where they set about making their fortunes.

Today a typical small western Malaysian town is an ethnic layer-cake. The two-storey, tile-roofed 'shophouses' lining the main street are Chinese. Their open-fronted ground floors are filled with goods that spill over onto the street – spice sacks, crates of soft drinks, baskets of betelnuts, lanterns, rice, noodles, brooms, mats, toys and perfumes.

When the sun becomes too strong, a bamboo awning is lowered, covered with beautifully written promises of the wonders within. Through the upstairs windows you may catch a glimpse of an old man reading a newspaper, or of children glued to a Cantonese videotape from Hong Kong. (*continued on p.103*)

This Iban chief's proud bearing is characteristic of his people. Arm, back and neck tattoos are still common among Dayak tribes.

Captain Bligh's bounty

The orchid family is considered by most botanists to be the largest, yet most vulnerable, family of flowering plants in the world, and it is also the most prized. Estimates of the number of orchid species worldwide vary considerably – from 17,000 to 30,000 – and such is the enthusiasm of the botanists that another 30,000 or so hybrids have been registered, with no end in sight. Malaysia can claim an especial richness in these wonderful plants, but here too as in the rest of the world they are under threat. With the Malaysian rainforests being felled at the rate of 30 acres a minute, thousands of rare species are endangered, or are already extinct.

Orchids were not always as widely known as they are nowadays – though tales of their glories did reach other parts of the world. Early European voyagers to Malaysia and surrounding lands returned home with glowing accounts of the strange and beautiful 'air plants' which grew on trees, but none of these wonders survived the journey home, and for many the tales were hard to believe. The first person to transport them successfully was the infamous Captain William Bligh (the *Bounty*'s captain at the time of its mutiny), who was responsible for bringing back most of the 15 different kinds of orchid that were cultivated at Kew Gardens in London in the 1770s.

After that, orchids became hugely popular as status symbols of the wealthy, and a flourishing and lucrative trade grew up in finding and exporting them to Europe. This was dominated by half a dozen enterprising London firms who dispatched scores of professional collectors to scour the tropics for new species. The competition was cut-throat. A collector might bag thousands of a single desirable species, then set the forest on fire to prevent a rival from collecting what was left. Often, the entire collection was lost on the long voyage home, in which case the man in the field would receive cabled instructions to 'return, re-collect'. The most intrepid were richly rewarded. As orchid-mania intensified, their discoveries fetched astounding prices at auction. Even then, losses were heavy, as Victorian horticulturists learned only slowly how to care for their exotic treasures, and England became

known for a time as,'the graveyard of the tropic orchid'.

In fact, orchids are prolific. Under the right conditions, they require little attention and flower profusely, and a Malay home will always have several in pots festooning the verandah. The hot and humid Malaysian forests yielded many beautiful specimens to the early hunters: *acanthophippium*, *aerides*, *arachnanthe*, *bulbophyllum*, *coelogyne* with slender and delicate blooms. Also *cymbidium*, the spectacular *dendrobium* with its frayed edges, *paphiopedilum* (ladies' slippers), and the delicately speckled *vanda* that Malays love to grow in their gardens.

Outside on the street, cooks in singlets and grubby shorts fry noodles at open stalls, while a Chinese opera singer wails out from a radio. Beyond the shophouses are the houses on stilts of the Malays, their fruit and flower gardens, rice paddies and rubber smallholdings. Beyond the town, on a big commercial plantation, the saris of the women and the brightly painted Hindu temple proclaim the origin of the work-gangs tending the rubber and palm oil trees. These people do not live in town, but in barracks on the plantation.

The shades of colonial Malaya are most lovingly conserved (with the benefits of tourism kept firmly in mind) up among the cool hill stations of the Cameron Highlands, where the families of the colonial officials and rubber planters of old used to escape the heat of summer. Nowadays, strawberries and cream and Olde English taverns are curious companions to Orang Asli tribesmen with blowpipes. And life is not always quite as safe as it seems. It was here in 1967 that the vacationing American silk magnate Jim Thompson disappeared while taking a pre-dinner stroll. Could it have been a tiger? The jungle is never very far away in Malaysia, and Kuala Lumpur gardens still harbour the odd cobra.

The KL experience

Kuala Lumpur means 'muddy estuary'. Two silt-laden rivers – the Gombak and the Klang – converge here, and so did a party of prospectors early in the tin boom. Although fever reduced their number to less than 20 in under a month, the survivors were successful enough for others to land their supplies and build huts here. Opium, gambling dens and brothels enlivened the mud patch, though perhaps not as much as the many murders and full-scale battles that erupted between rival clans and became known collectively as the Wars of the Chinese Miners.

KL (as everyone affectionately calls it) was still a ramshackle jungle outpost under a Chinese headman known as Kapitan China when the British took control in 1885. They immediately built a rail line to the coast and, by the end of the century, KL was the colonial capital; it is now both the federal capital of Malaysia and its business centre.

KL is the sum of the Malaysian experience and is therefore South-East Asia at its most varied: a more attractive city to live in, some say, than to visit. Sharp-edged towers of steel and glass look down upon a large and clamorous Chinatown, while mosques and Hindu temples nudge old colonial edifices ranging in style from mock-Tudor to a Supreme Court building worthy of the Arabian nights. The national mosque (its dome crowned with 18 stars, which represent the five fundamental principles of Islam and the thirteen constituent states of federal Malaysia) is almost jarringly modernistic, while the railway station standing close by is an exuberant Victorian fantasy of minarets and arches.

At the city's heart, the Selangor Club still looks out over the *Padang* (green), much as it did at midnight on August 30, 1957, when the Union Jack was lowered here for the last time, on the occasion of Malaysia's independence from Britain. They still play cricket on the *Padang*, but players of every creed and colour, like the club membership of senior government officials and a multi-hued business elite, reflect a very different world from that of the whisky-sipping officers and gentlemen of colonial days.

To the south, the National Museum (Muzim Negara) provides an excellent introduction to the country as a whole. It is housed in an enlarged version of a traditional Malay village home. Among the exhibits in the cultural gallery are the leather wayang kulit shadow puppets used by village storytellers to act out folk stories.

Styles in KL's teeming streets are a study in diversity. Some of the men wear T-shirts, while others are impeccably turned out in the suits and ties that are the uniform of all ambitious young executives. Women wear a whole range of clothes: blouses with batik sarongs; Western-style dresses; Chinese dresses, known as *samfoos*; filmy pastel saris; or black trousers and slit-sided tops.

The diversity of the city's fare, meanwhile, is best experienced on Petaling Street, where traffic is banned from 6pm – at which point of the day hundreds of mobile kitchens are rolled out and tables set up. All kinds of delicacies are soon sizzling and bubbling under the bright acetylene lamps: charcoal-grilled satay meat sticks with sweet and spicy sauce, oily fritters dripping with sugar, dumplings and sweet breads filled

The palm wine-maker has to scale a palm tree with a machete. At the top, he makes an incision in the heart of the tree and positions a bottle beneath the gash to collect the sap. Next day, he climbs back to empty the contents of the bottle into a can. The uninitiated consider the product relatively drinkable when fresh but dreadful once it starts to ferment.

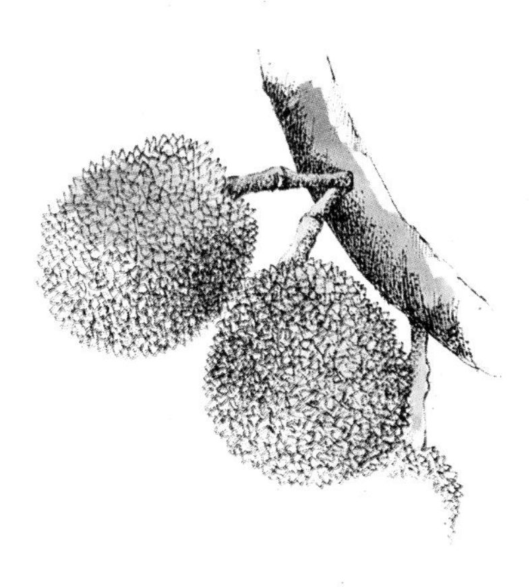

The spiky-skinned durian is notorious for its pungent odour, which has been likened to over-ripe cheese or an open sewer. Malays find its creamy white pulp delectable, and it is rumoured to be both an aphrodisiac, and a favourite with tigers. Europeans are not so sure, but Charles Darwin swore that it was worth going around the world for.

Rubber collectors must be grateful that their trees can be tapped from the bottom. The white latex oozes slowly into a little cup from a slanted incision that is regularly reopened to allow daily collection. Trees are productive for 30 to 35 years.

with bean paste and chicken curry, *dim sum* and roast duck, and specialities from every corner of China; or banana leaf curries, *biryanis* and *murtabaks,* stuffed *rotis,* and all the dishes of India, from the subtle flavours of the north to the chili-hot south.

Sellers of everything and nothing hawk their wares through the drifting crowds. Healers, Chinese or Indian, set out their miracle potions at street corners and make magic passes over half-naked patients, while onlookers stand around and gawk. Girls dressed in black satin, their hair and faces made up the European way, sell their knowledgeable charms. At dawn, the aroma of bakeries fills the air, and housewives are up early to forage among the freshly-piled vegetables and pyramids of exotic fruits. As the city springs to life, traffic surges down Jalan Petaling, and the street takes on yet another aspect, as the expensive limousines of impatient Chinese industrialists and European managers battle with the dense throngs of bicycles and trishaws in a blare of horns and bells.

The babble is indescribable, for each person appears to be speaking in a different tongue. Even now, several Chinese dialects are spoken in Malaysia, so no two Chinese necessarily understand each other. It is the same for the Indians. But when it comes to trading and the exciting ritual of bargaining, the language of money is understood by all.

Kuantan, capital of the east coast state of Pahang, is celebrated for its woodcarving, weaving, brocade and batik while, in the adjoining village of Selamat, silk sarongs are handwoven with strange and intricate designs in gold and silver thread. Many of the craft shops are Indian-owned. The beauty of these artefacts is no less impressive for having to share space with fruits, sweets, newspapers and magazines.

Sons of the soil

The Japanese invaders took only 54 days in December 1941 and January 1942 to advance the length of the Malay peninsula, in tanks and on bicycles, and 15 more to capture Singapore, the island at its tip that had become the key British bastion in the East. In the process, the Japanese lost 15,000 men, while the defenders lost over ten times as many: an estimated 166,600 men.

Britain's prestige never recovered from this helter-skelter rout. Anti-colonial sentiment had in any case been growing in the peninsula during the 1920s and 30s, influenced in large measure by the example of India's nationalists. The Japanese invasion showed that Westerners were by no means invincible, and within 10 years of the end of the Second World War, peninsular Malaya was assured full self-rule, with the redoubtable Malay nationalist, Tunku Abdul Rahman, as its most forceful leader. By 1965, the enlarged

Federation of Malaysia had attained its present size and form, as a parliamentary democracy with a uniquely rotating monarchy, the *agong* (or king) being chosen every five years from among nine state sultans.

Malaysia has been called an 'anthropological museum' of a nation, since nothing of its past appears to have been lost. Small, timid bands of aboriginal negrito people still hunt and gather in the remote corners where their ancestors were pushed millennia ago ... tribes identified as of proto-Malaysian origin ... proud Malay-Chinese descended from early Ming adventurers ... Chinese of more recent vintage ... Malaysians of Portuguese descent still faithful to their Catholic heritage and antique Portuguese dialect ... and so it goes on.

Unfortunately, there is a snag. The spectre of Chinese domination has haunted the Malays since before independence, and was an important factor in the failure of the (predominantly Chinese) Communist uprising in 1948. It was also the reason behind Singapore's expulsion from the Federation, since Singapore is overwhelmingly Chinese. Malays made up half the population of Malaysia, but had less than 2 per cent of the wealth, when race riots in 1969 provoked a drastic policy response. Ethnic Malays and indigenous tribespeople were classified as *bumipatra*, or 'sons of the soil', and they began to benefit from positive discrimination in both education and job opportunities, while businesses were obliged to allot part of their capital to *bumipatras*.

Results were mixed. A Malay middle-class was certainly created, but after 20 years, the *bumipatras* still lagged well behind the Chinese in wealth, and critics accused a small ruling cartel of prospering in their name. There was also bitterness among the Indians and Chinese, not least for being called 'immigrants' in a land they had inhabited for several generations. From the other flank, a rise in Islamic fundamentalism threatened stability.

Nothing is tastier to a Malaysian than a dish of fat grasshoppers lightly grilled and then sautéed in a pan. Supplied live in a net, they are awkward to sell without substantial losses!

Kota Belud, in Sabah, is famous for its colourful tamu *(market meeting place) and irrepressible Badjau market women. The Badjau, sea gypsies originally from across the Sula Sea and now also noted horse-breeders, live in stilt villages built entirely over the water.*

Happy New Year... New Year... New Year...

One benefit of such a fractured society is the multiplicity of reasons for celebration. This is the country in which New Year – Hindu, Chinese, Muslim and Western – comes around four times a year! And with Muslims, Hindus and Chinese all timing their holy happenings by different lunar calendars, the kaleidoscope of events gets shaken into a spectacular and ever-changing pattern.

By far the most spectacular is the ceremony of Thaipusam, on the Hindu day of atonement – an occasion for such masochistic excesses that it is – officially at least – banned in India. Up to 300,000 chanting devotees of the Lord Subramaniam, son of the god Shiva, invade the streets of Kuala Lumpur by night, and march in a dawn procession to the Batu Caves. This vast natural cathedral in a limestone outcrop is only seven miles from the city, but was hidden by the jungle until modern times. During the Second World War, Communist guerrillas fighting the Japanese occupation forces used the caves as a hideout, and when Hindu worshippers set up a shrine here, pilgrims had to scale a precipitous cliff-face to reach their goal. Now a stepped concrete causeway carries the human wave up and into the mouth of the cave.

Hundreds of the most devout, or desperate, penitents are clad only in a white loin cloth. They carry the *kavadi,* heavy wooden or metal chokers laden with flowers, fruits and ritual objects, which are suspended from their bodies by metal spikes, super-sized needles and grappling hooks driven through the flesh. The most devout of all pierce their tongues with skewers and walk on sandals of nails. They have fasted for a month, sitting cross-legged in temples, and have chewed betelnut all night, with the result that their saliva looks like blood oozing from the mouth. Drums and chants of *'vel ... vel'* (victory) propel them onwards. Many are in a deep trance by the time they reach the Lord Subramaniam, enthroned in bejewelled effigy in a glowing grotto; white-robed priests sprinkle sacred ash on their bodies and remove their burdens.

Lights, fires, shadows, chanting, the scent of camphor and sanpagita flowers, and the press of excited people: everything contributes to the mystery of this extraordinary ceremony. Similar rites take place in Penang, in a bat-filled cave where snakes provide an added hazard. Something of a tourist attraction, these temple asps become so drowsed from incense and sated with offerings that they can be safely photographed close up.

Deepavali is very different: the festival of light, when Hindus celebrate Lord Krishna's victory over evil is in a way quite similar to Christmas. Indeed, Christmas lights are now generally preferred to the traditional oil lamps, and since Christmas itself is not far off, many Indian shops keep their decorations up for their

Like a human pin-cushion, this Thaipusam penitent hopes to obtain absolution for his sins and gain the good will of the Hindu gods by loading himself with offerings suspended from his flesh by large hooks and spikes.

About 10 per cent of Malays are of Indian origin. Most of their forebears were Tamils from the south of India, hired as contract labour on the tea and rubber plantations of colonial Malaya. Some remain poor agricultural workers, but others have made their mark in the professions, or have good government posts.

The trishaw, or bicycle rickshaw, is an agreeable way to get around Malaysian cities, and much less alarming than the ride provided by the country's suicidally fast taxi drivers. The trishaw rider may look put-upon while taking his siesta, but he is an astute businessman, renowned for hard bargaining with the solicitous tourist.

Hitched to the tip of the Malay peninsula by a causeway, the mini-state of Singapore is the second-busiest port in the world and the financial and industrial hub of South-East Asia. In 1819, when the visionary Sir Stamford Raffles selected it to be Britain's 'great commercial emporium' in the East, it was nothing but jungle and swamp infested by tigers, crocodiles, and pirates.

Christian customers, and sometimes for the Chinese New Year as well!

As good Muslims, Malays observe Ramadan, the 30 days during which they may not eat or drink from sunrise to sunset. On Hari Raya, day of the celebration at the end of Ramadan, it is their turn to throw a big party to which other races are invited. Since theirs is the state religion, the birthday of Mohammed is a national holiday, when mosques and their forecourts are decorated with banners and resound to prayers and chanting. When night falls, it is time for long walks and long chats among friends over *satay* and soft drinks, music, dancing and fireworks.

Compared to the mosques, with calls to prayer five times a day from every minaret, the red-and-gold, black-and-gold Chinese temples seem so still and quiet: their only signs of life, the smoke trails from incense sticks drifting lazily up towards the muffled sound of a gong, or the tinkle of small bells, high in the roof. Taoist or Buddhist, the Chinese have a private way of practising their complex religion, with its emphasis on the quest for good fortune.

But do not be fooled by this: at the very least excuse – be it wedding, birth or burial – they spill outdoors in noisy and extravagant demonstrations. Purple, white and pale blue banners are unfurled, and candles placed on street altars. The tables are then set and loaded with whole roasted and glazed piglets and other foods. The din of live and canned music becomes deafening, and actors appear, heavily made up and dressed in purple and gold. A curtain, footlights and a trailer for the back-stage are soon in place, and the street becomes an opera house. Though everyone knows every story by heart, the audience will watch with rapt attention for as many hours as it takes the performers to re-enact some classic tale in the classic way, to the rhythmic accompaniment of gong and cymbal.

Practically every day in the Taoist-Buddhist calendar has some cause for a feast; very often it is the birthday of a deity. Ghosts are the focus of the Yulan festival, when food is set out for wandering spirits, and paper houses, motor cars and imitation bank notes are burned as offerings to them. Lately, some lucky spirits have even been in receipt of credit cards.

You do not have to be Chinese to enjoy a Chinese festival, and the entire population looks forward to the Chinese New Year, at the end of January or early February, with Christmas serving as a mini-rehearsal for the celebration to come. This is when the hard-working Chinese really let go, with a release of decibels that deafens the whole nation.

Dragon and lion dances and parades mark the start of the celebrations. The head of the dragon is made from papier mache, and several dancers are concealed under its long, caterpillar-like body, which is made of cloth. The lions guard the temples – they are half-ferocious, half-funny monsters, inhabited by two or more dancers, who wheel madly about, snapping their jaws and flapping their eyelids in time to the loud clash of cymbals.

Youngsters receive *ang pows,* gifts of money in red packets, lucky mottos and the astrological sign of the year appears everywhere, painted in gold on red paper. There is much visiting and much eating, and everybody is wished a Kong Hee Fatt Choy – a happy and prosperous new year.

Hari Raya, Fatt Choy, Deepavali – the great feasts can last for days. Rather than declarations of difference, each provides an opportunity for a sector to play host to the rest of this complicated plural society, and to foster together tolerance and understanding.

Indonesia

Few travellers fail to be captivated by Indonesia's charms.
And few fail to be baffled by its diversity. It is truly a land of
superlatives, consisting of 13,677 islands, huge and tiny,
scattered over more than 3 million square miles of the Earth's
surface, and with at least 100 active volcanoes.
Matching the riches of its scenery are the riches of its
peoples and cultures, ranging from the once-cannibal
Bataks of Sumatra to the sophisticated Hindu civilisation of Bali
to the entirely individual traditions of the Toraja 'men of the
mountains' of Sulawesi.

The boy on the buffalo rides his steed with a skill born of confidence. The docile nature of the beast makes it a perfect play partner.

***Previous page:** The seas teem with fish, but most Javanese are loath to venture upon them, tending only to fish on a small scale. Japan scoops up the windfall, and sells the Indonesians their own harvest.*

This village beneath Java's Mount Bromo is under constant threat, so the villagers make offerings to placate the fire god. Observances include an annual pilgrimage to the top of the volcano.

Java: Under the Volcanoes

It is a clear morning, and the sun is still low on the horizon. A solitary, misty cloud hugs the gigantic cone of Gunung Merapi. It is rice-planting time, and the entire family is in the paddy, wading in the mud. Ahead lie eight to ten back-breaking hours, meticulously planting the tiny seedlings which, in a few weeks, will each grow into a splendid green plant, turning golden as they ripen. The soil here is the most fertile on earth.

Suddenly, an explosion tears the sky apart. The father straightens, and looks towards the volcano. The top of the cone has vanished, vaporised. A few moments pass before the shock wave reaches the paddy field, and the ground trembles. Darkness descends, illuminated where a flow of incandescent lava spills down the mountainside. Three days later, the lava is cooling along a swathe of devastation more than a mile wide and 20 miles long; there are 200 dead, and 10,000 homeless. Such is the price of fertility in Java.

Blazing mountains

Gunung Merapi – 'the blazing mountain' – is one among more than 400 volcanoes which stretch in a line through Sumatra, Java, Bali, to Sulawesi and Maluku. Most of the hundred or so volcanoes that have been active in the past still are. One of them produced the biggest bang in recorded history. On August 23, 1883, the island volcano of Krakatoa, lying between Java and Sumatra, blew up, hurling five cubic miles of mountain and molten magma 17 miles into the air.

The explosion was heard 3000 miles away. Debris blocked the strait between Java and Sumatra, and the ash in the atmosphere drifted three times around the world, filtering out sunlight and chilling the global climate for two years. Two-thirds of Krakatoa sank beneath enormous tidal waves that also drowned thousands of people on other islands. In 1928, a small volcano rose from the water, and was duly named Anak Krakatoa, Son of Krakatoa.

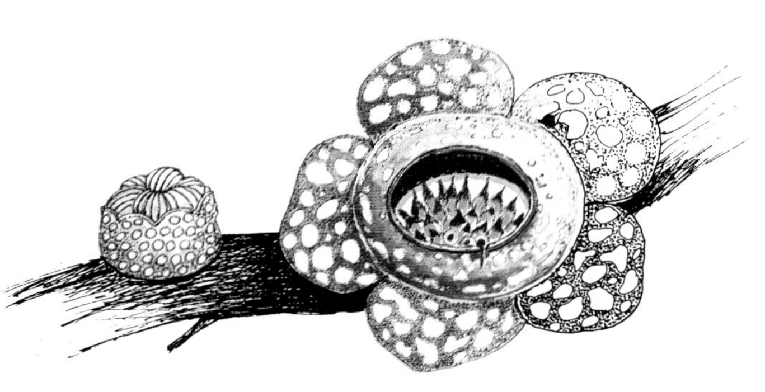

The rafflesia of central Sumatra is the world's largest flower, with blooms measuring 3 feet across. The plant is a parasite growing on trees and is named after Sir Stamford Raffles, founder of Singapore, who spent several years in Sumatra.

Java is the epicentre of all this fire and smoke: more than a third of all active volcanoes on earth are hissing and spluttering on this island the size of Britain. It is a hothouse in every sense; its tropical rainforests are the most luxuriant on the planet – or they were, before mankind came and cut them down. In Java, even the fence-posts will sprout roots and start to grow. From the dawn of history, this extraordinary fertility has made Java the most coveted of islands: the cradle of the region's civilisations and hub of its religions.

In the 14th century, the Majapahit kings of Java claimed sovereignty over the Indonesian archipelago. Six hundred years later, in August 1945, the smoke of the Second World War cleared sufficiently to reveal the red and white *Merdeka* (freedom) flag fluttering over the island. There were well over a quarter of a million

Tea plantations flank twisting Puncak Pass, between Jakarta and Bandung. The young woman plucks the fragile stem tips with speed and dexterity.

Japanese occupation forces still concentrated on Java, and almost as many interned Dutch eager to reclaim their colony. British-Indian forces landed to try to contain the situation. During 1946 Dutch forces arrived and took over. However, the force of Indonesian nationalism forced the Dutch to give in. At the end of 1949 the Dutch East Indies became the independent Republic of Indonesia.

Java and the Javanese dominate what is now a nation of more than 13,000 islands – 3000 of them inhabited – spreading 3000 miles from the Asian mainland into the Pacific. 'They are many; they are one,' was a saying from Majapahit times that was turned into a motto for the new nation: 'Unity in Diversity'. Although about 85 per cent are nominally Muslim and predominantly of Malay extraction, this seeming uniformity obscures as many cultural fault-lines as the geology. Java alone is home to several ethnic groups, the Javanese themselves being only one. Faith in Allah likewise forks many ways, between the orthodox *santri* and the majority *abangan*, who blend Islam with Hindu-Buddhist traditions and animistic nature worship.

The new state sought to keep everyone content (but angered fundamentalist Muslims) by affirming official belief in an unspecified 'God', who was symbolised on the coat of arms by a star. To unite this nation that speaks some 250 different languages, the government pressed forward with the universal teaching of *Bahasa Indonesia*, a form of Malay first used by traders, as an official language. Unfortunately, *Merdeka* zeal took a militaristic turn, and the domination of the army in domestic and business affairs was accompanied by mismanagement and corruption which reached a dismal climax when Pertamina, the national oil company (headed by a general), collapsed with debts of over 10 billion dollars, or more than the national budget!

Batik, Java's best-known craft product, requires a deft hand and infinite patience. The worker cannot stray a fraction from the intricate design as she applies hot wax to the cloth. When the cloth is dyed, a pattern is created around the areas protected by the wax layer. The wax is removed, and the cloth washed clean before fresh wax is applied according to another element of the design. Then the cloth is dyed a second colour – and so on, until the desired effect is achieved. As many as eight colours may be applied, involving weeks of work.

Squalor and wealth

The other problem relates to Java alone. It was believed to be over-populated in 1850, when the population was 10 million. Now it is 110 million. Java, with seven per cent of the land area, is home to two out of every three Indonesians. It is twice as densely populated as any other territory of comparable size in the world. Seen from the air, human activity holds the mountains in a tight choke. Each year, the population increases by 2 to 3 million, and the choke tightens. Near the historic court city of Yogyakatra (Jogya) on Mount Merapi's southern slopes, even rural population densities can reach 5000 to the square mile.

The Dutch used to remove people to less populous islands, and *transmigrasi* – transmigration – is still being tried. Enticements bordering on coercion are used to encourage people to leave Java for Sumatra, Sulawesi and elsewhere. Plans called for the shifting of more than 5 million people by the early 1990s, but the effect

is at best minimal. Local people are suspicious of what they see as Javanese colonisation of the outer islands, and many 'pioneers' slip back to Java, where they join a growing, resentful sub-proletariat. Java's cities are several times the size they were at the time of independence, and there is a considerable middle class living in vast housing estates. Filth and squalor rub shoulders with the wealth of a minority. The recyclers of cigarette butts can hope to earn in a week what the rich spend on a single bunch of imported grapes.

All these problems are most acutely noticeable in the capital Jakarta (the old Dutch Batavia). Nobody knows exactly how many people live there, but the correct figure is probably in the region of 13 million if its sprawling outer rim is taken into account. And here again the contrasts are disturbing. Strolling along the wide, modern streets of the Menteng district, you might imagine yourself at the heart of a city of Western affluence. Immaculately dressed women pop in and out of smart boutiques, while limousines pull up in front of the Indonesian headquarters of most of the world's major banks and multinational corporations, disgorging severely suited businessmen.

And yet, just a few blocks to the north or east, and you are in a different world altogether. Narrow streets are a thronged and noisy mass of pedestrians, ancient hooting motor cars and innumerable *bajajs* (basically, motor scooters with room for two passengers up behind) and *becaks* (bicycle rickshaws). Farther out again, and you reach bleak expanses of shanty towns which house the thousands of immigrants who pour into Jakarta each year from the rest of Indonesia.

Symbolic of it all is the 433-foot, Russian-built National Monument which rises from the central Merdeka Square. This is topped by a sculpted flame – the flame of Indonesia's freedom – coated with 77 pounds of pure gold. It was the World Bank which gave the Indonesian state the money to buy the gold ... while so many Indonesian people were living on, or below, the bread line.

The entire village joins in harvesting one family's rice paddy. Speed is important, since the crop could be ruined by a few days' delay. In order to minimise risk, the villagers grow their rice on a staggered rotation, with paddies ripening a few days apart. Centuries of team effort instil a strong community spirit.

Village life

For the peasant families on the land, not very much has changed since the days of the Dutch, except that their growing numbers oblige them to move ever further up the mountains, closer to the cones of death. The typical family home has only one room, shared by as many as four generations. The family keeps itself to itself, cultivating its small plot of land, inherited or won from the mountain. But what land! It will produce rice, coffee, tea, tobacco, cloves, pepper, peanuts and all sorts of spices with equal facility, without resort to fertilisers or pesticide. It never seems to wear out. A family of 15 to 20 can thrive on the yield of less than an acre – which is just as well, since there is hardly enough regular, paid work for a quarter of Java's population.

As in all equatorial countries, the rhythm of life is set by *matahari* – eye of the day – the sun. The village wakes at 5am, and by 6am about 100 women in cotton sarongs are settled among carefully arranged wicker baskets of produce in what passes for the village square, but is really a gap between two houses. The trading is relaxed and jovial, and accompanied by much eloquently expressive gesturing. Here is a corner piled with exotic fruits; there are stacks of fragrant spices; and right next to them, you will find the bird market: no home is complete without its bird cage, its captive occupant a Javanese symbol of freedom. Blessed with such a cornucopia of fruit and vegetables, the Javanese enjoy meat, and *satays* sizzle on skewers in the market's little open-air cafe. Strategically positioning himself between meat and bird sections, a 'doctor' dispenses advice and dubious-looking medicines: the *dukun*, sorcerer-doctor-astrologer-psychotherapist-seer, would never miss the morning market.

Food is not all that the village produces. Much of Java's most famous export, its batik cloth, is produced in village workshops, where women toil tirelessly at the many cycles of waxing and dyeing required to create the beautiful multi-colour effects. Meanwhile, the men tend the fields. At daybreak, the landscape is dotted with thousands of bent silhouettes, floating ghost-like in the fine mist. The sun burns off the mist, and details are sharply etched against the dark, lowering mass of the volcano: clumps of palm, fragile homesteads, files of buffalo carts. Work in the fields stops at 11am, when the heat becomes unbearable. Activity resumes at 3pm, and culminates with a bath at the village waterhole.

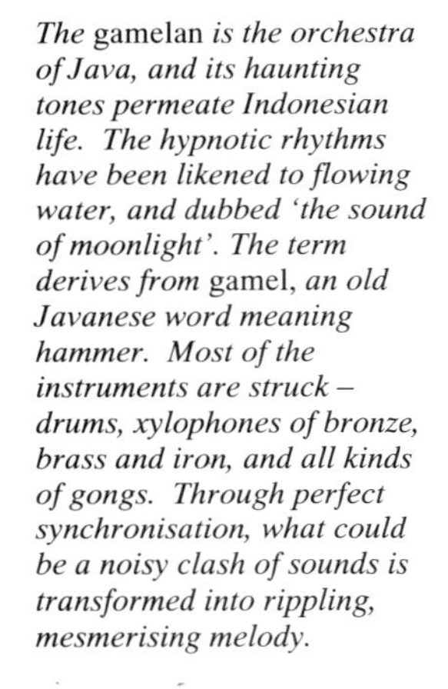

The gamelan *is the orchestra of Java, and its haunting tones permeate Indonesian life. The hypnotic rhythms have been likened to flowing water, and dubbed 'the sound of moonlight'. The term derives from* gamel, *an old Javanese word meaning hammer. Most of the instruments are struck – drums, xylophones of bronze, brass and iron, and all kinds of gongs. Through perfect synchronisation, what could be a noisy clash of sounds is transformed into rippling, mesmerising melody.*

At night, the village may find release in the world of *wayang*, as it is transported to a long-ago Java by a solitary figure squatting cross-legged on a mat before a white screen lit by an oil lamp. The *wayang* shadow plays are Java's most visible link with its pre-Islamic past, and go to the core of the highly mystical Javanese soul. They are mostly based on the Hindu epics, and a single story can last all through the night, narrated and chanted by the *dalang* (puppet master) to the haunting accompaniment of a *gamelan* orchestra consisting of an assortment of gongs, drums and xylophones.

Living beneath their volcanoes has made the Javanese more ready than most people to believe in magic and sorcery. Amulets or musical instruments are regularly credited with magical powers, and a *kris* invariably so. The long dagger with the distinctive wavy blade has fascinated the Javanese for centuries. A Javanese will tell you that two *krises* placed in the same box will fight; that a *kris* may leave its scabbard at night and kill; that it knows good from evil, and may exact justice on its own account.

In Java, a sense of the mystical goes all the way to the top. President Suharto was raised in the home of a *dukun* (medicine man), and is said to identify with Semar, a popular *wayang* god noted for saving tricky situations. Suharto even sometimes goes off to meditate in a mountain cave that is said to be Semar's dwelling-place.

Backed by a gamelan *orchestra, the* wayang kulit *puppeteer, or* dalang, *puts on a virtuoso performance that can last from dusk to dawn.* Wayang *means shadow, or ghost, and* kulit *means leather. The highly stylised figures are delicately chiselled out of buffalo hide and mounted on horn rods (opposite below). Good characters are placed on the right, evil on the left. The* dalang *not only manipulates the figures, but also narrates, and speaks all the parts. The audience sits in the dark behind a white cotton screen, and sees the action as a shadow play.* Wayang *drama has been popular for almost a thousand years. In western Java, the same plays are performed with* wayang golek, *three-dimensional puppets worked by rods.*

The bull races of Madura

Madura Island, tucked into north-east Java, breeds bold men and fine cattle, a combination which has resulted in the unique sport of bull racing. What began as a casual contest between plough teams galumphing the length of a rice field is now a highly organised competition lasting from mid-August to the September grand finals in Pamekasan, the Madura capital. The bulls are specially bred, and conditioned on a diet of beer, honey, raw eggs and chili.

Racing bulls operate on much the same principle as motor-racing dragsters, only the risks are double, since they are hitched together in pairs. The dare-devil jockey perches on a trailing sleigh between the tails of his team as they accelerate down the straight. Finalists are led to the stadium in ribbons, flowers, even make-up. Cheers, drums, gongs and craftily slipped shots of arak send them bolting down the track, and sometimes into the over-excited spectators, at speeds approaching 30mph.

This quiet waterscape is 2600 feet above sea level, in the heart of Sumatra's Batak country. Lake Toba is larger (660 square miles) and deeper (1500 feet) than any other body of fresh water in South-East Asia. Head-hunting was once a Batak social problem; now the problem is tourism.

'Orang-utan' means 'man of the forest' in Malay. The big tree-dwelling ape with the curiously human expression is gentle and peaceful – too much so for its own good. It breeds infrequently, is easily captured, and is doomed to extinction unless current rescue efforts are successful.

Sumatra: Island of Surprises

About 100 people are gathered at the base of the great house: family, friends, the whole village. All eyes are trained intently on a narrow door under the eaves of the thatched roof.

A girl appears, smiling shyly in her ceremonial dress, holding a baby in her arms. Flustered, yet proud, impeded by her tight skirt and her precious burden, she gingerly clambers down the steps, and sets the baby on the ground. Everybody cheers. The baby was born over a month ago, and now the mother has performed the ritual of 'bringing to the ground'; according to the rites of her people, she is purified, and the child has joined the community of the Batak, a mountain race from northern Sumatra. It is time to feast!

Lush storehouse

Sumatra is in geological torment. The earth's crust has reared and buckled, torn and sheared in creating the country's 1000-mile spine of high ridge studded with volcanoes; this is sheer on the western face and then descends through rolling hills on the other flank to malarial mangrove swamps. At 195,000 square miles, it is the fifth-largest island in the world – about the size of Sweden or California. Sumatra straddles the Equator, nudging Malaysia along the narrow Malacca Strait, and nosing up to Java.

It is incredibly lush. 'Put a stick into our earth and it will grow' is a saying among the Minang people of west Sumatra. A hundred species of trees and plants can sometimes be found within a single acre of the island's rainforests, which are also home to the elusive Sumatran tiger and the last few, gentle orang-utans. The swamps and jungles of the eastern province of Riau, meanwhile, are home to the 100 or so surviving Sumatran rhinos. Unlike their African cousins, these rhinos are comparatively small – 9 feet long at most – and hairy. Marco Polo saw one when he visited Sumatra in 1292 on a journey from China to Persia, and thought he had stumbled across a real-life specimen of the mythical unicorn.

In ways other than geographical, Sumatra forms Indonesia's backbone – there is oil here; this is where Shell had its origins a century ago, and since then finds have been made all along the island's east coast. Sumatra's oil, together with the abundant crops of rubber, tea, coffee, tobacco and palm oil produced in its alluvial north-east corner, is what keeps all of Indonesia going. This north-east part of the island was also the scene of some of the worst excesses of the colonial regime. Dutch plantation managers in the late 19th century were effectively a law unto themselves and imposed extremely harsh working conditions, using their 'coolie' labourers from Java or southern China as little better than slaves. Flogging was a regular punishment and many of the labourers died as a result of deficiencies in their diet – a single outbreak of beri beri (caused by a lack of vitamin B) wiped out nearly 80 per cent of the work force in the 1880s.

Rubber is one of the main products of a fertile region in north-east Sumatra, exploited by Dutch and British planters in the 19th century. Tapping rubber trees for their sap provides welcome work for some of Indonesia's army of unemployed, but the country does not have the technology or the large amounts of energy required to process the raw material into finished products: a familiar problem in the developing world.

The manufacture of rubber requires energy and skill – which are not always available in Indonesia. The country can cope with the preparation of the raw material but not some of the later stages needed to finish the product: a fact which deprives Indonesia of some of the added value.

Fundamentalists and mother figures

Sumatra is a storehouse of another kind. As both a barrier and gateway between the Pacific and Indian Oceans, it straddles a major world trade route. Control of the Malacca and Sunda Straits was as crucial in the Second World War as it was 1300 years earlier, when the fabled Buddhist kingdom of Sriwijaya prospered by controlling the flow of trade through these two choke-points. Because of this crossroads location, and because its mountains and swamps made penetration difficult, Sumatra accumulated a rich variety of migrant cultures that, once settled, tended to develop in mutual isolation.

The range extends from fiercely proud Muslim fundamentalists to the world's largest surviving matrilineal society. The route of all intrusion – Hindus, Buddhists, Muslims, Portuguese, English, Dutch – was through the north coast, where the Acehnese are living evidence of the country's ethnic diversity: a mix of Malay, Indian, Arab, Javanese, Chinese and who-knows-what-besides, they found unity in fiercely upholding the faith of the Prophet and defying the Dutch to the death. Attacked by 10,000 Dutch forces in 1873, they exacted terrible losses in a long *jihad* (holy war), and as a result of their continuing tradition of independence have been accorded a degree of autonomy from Jakarta.

The Minangkabau of the foothills of the south-west (around Padang) are Muslim too, yet they have preserved an ancient system of matriliny, even in the face of bloody warfare in the 19th century, when fanatical pilgrims returned from Mecca with a determination to correct the deviant ways of their people. Property and social responsibility revolve strictly around the woman, not the man. A big Minangkabau longhouse (*rumah gadang*) may be home to several families, all of them descended from one ancestral mother.

Everyone belongs for life to his or her maternal *rumah*. In hindering the private accumulation of wealth, the Minangkabau inheritance laws have also hindered the fragmentation of landholding, and the combined resources of large kin groups have resulted in economic success in the wider world. Far from being cultural curiosities, the Minangkabau have a high literacy rate and a reputation for managerial skill; they were at the forefront of the independence movement, and many of Indonesia's leading politicians, writers and intellectuals have been Minang.

Wedged between the Acehnese and the Minang around Lake Toba are the Batak, whose existence was first revealed to an incredulous outside world by an 18th-century account of the discovery of a cannibal kingdom that was nevertheless cultured and literate. The Batak do not eat people any more, but they still take pride in being different.

This Minangkabau lady is lord of her domain, and her husband a beggar in his own home! The Minangkabau are the world's largest matrilineal society: property is passed down the female line; families are headed by their eldest female member; and fathers have limited say in family affairs. The system works admirably. Able, restless, with a sophsticated culture, the Minangkabau are one of Indonesia's most prosperous people.

The Minangkabau claim descent from Alexander the Great. The origin of their name is uncertain, but they prefer an explanation as romantic as the Alexander story. Long, long ago, they were threatened by a powerful Javanese king. To avoid bloodshed, they got the king to agree to let their best buffaloes fight it out. The Javanese selected a splendid beast. The Sumatrans picked a young calf, starved it for several days and stuck a sharp spike on its nose. Frantic for milk, the calf took the big buffalo to be its mother and, rushing under its belly, jabbed it so painfully that it took flight. Thereupon, the Sumatrans all shouted 'minang kabau!', which roughly translates as 'our buffalo wins'. Together with this cry, they adopted the distinctive headdress to commemorate for ever their clever victory.

Through the green tunnel

The Trans-Sumatra Highway starts from the great port of Medan in the north, and snakes upwards through jungle-smothered hills in which the foliage is so deep and dense that it is like driving through a green tunnel. The Karo Batak dwell in these hills. A short distance from the road, though obscured from it, a Karo village nestles under great trees: a dozen houses on piles arranged around a courtyard, their huge thatched roofs reaching almost to the ground; each has only a tiny door and two small windows to let in minimal light. An unexpected visit is liable to bring about mass desertion, with everyday objects left scattered by the residents in their haste to flee the approach of the stranger. Mistrust, and an obsession for seclusion, are characteristics of forest people.

A few miles further on, the road rises again. The forest thins, giving way to great oaks and laurel, then to true mountain vegetation. The road bends, and a huge expanse of bright blue-green water springs into view. Lake Toba is the lovely consequence of an eruption

The uncertain quality of this rice harvest in Batak country suggests that the land will shortly be rested. Fresh jungle – perhaps the patch just beyond the Toba village – will be cleared as a replacement. The line of banana trees fringing the village is important as a source of food – and is also all that is required for periodic house maintenance.

50,000 years ago that must have had the explosive power of many Krakatoas, since it blew out an 800 square mile caldera. The crater lake is big enough comfortably to contain a 25 mile by 12 mile island lying at its centre: this is Samosir, lovely 'homeland' of the Toba Batak.

The name 'Batak' is thought to derive from a Malay term for robber or blackmailer, or it might have originated as a Muslim expression of scorn, roughly equivalent to 'pig-eater'. There are more than 3 million Batak, divided into six tribes with different dialects and customs. Their ancestors are thought to have migrated from the foothills of the Himalayas. They must have found just what they were looking for in the Sumatran mountains, for nothing could make them budge or take to their neighbours' ways for the following 1500 years. When the Dutch first stumbled upon them, the Batak were a most sophisticated society of headhunters.

The Batak organise themselves in precisely the opposite manner to that of their neighbours the Minangkabau. Social organisation is based on the man, everyone belonging to the family clan of their father;

women do not count. Genealogies dating back 500 years are kept, with the result that 1000 or more relatives are liable to turn up for a wedding or funeral.

Until recently village design reflected the warlike past, and communities are surrounded by a moat, wall or palisade, with a single entrance. The houses are in line, and face a row of rice barns. The chief's house (*sopo*) is taller and larger, and doubles as the meeting house; the chief dispenses justice in cases of customary law (*adat*), but decisions affecting the community are reached by general agreement.

Like the Minang, the Batak build massively elegant multi-family wooden homes on stilts, with tall, pointed thatched roofs that sink in the middle to give the effect of a high-prowed boat, or a set of buffalo horns. The gables are decorated with frightening sculptures of bug-eyed monsters and serpents, painted in the holy colours of red for the benevolent gods, white for the forces of nature, and black for the earth spirits. Stairs under the house lead up through a trap door to the interior, which is a single large room in which four to five families live. It is dark, almost pitch black, and filled with acrid smoke. About 20 people gather round the hearth, where rice cakes are cooked, and pieces of pork fried in oil that has been used a thousand times; a pot of vegetables

In Batak country, styles can change in just a few miles, as this classically Karo structure demonstrates. Part of a reconstruction of the royal village of Pematang Purba, it is being preserved as a living museum of Batak tradition. Families directly descended from tribal royalty live in the village and skilfully perpetuate old crafts.

The quality of votive decorative sculpture on the Karo house posts compares badly with the intricate detailing in Minangkabau country, and is visual testimony to the problems of the region.

boils gently on the side of the fire, and a plate of rice rests at the centre of the hearth. There is palm wine fermented in bamboo, and a white, tart beer that leaves bad memories if too much is drunk.

The thirteenth moon

In a small gallery built into the roof, an ageless man silently contemplates the goings-on in the common room below. He is the village chief, also its wise man and holder of the Batak calendar. The Batak year is divided into 12 months with a total of no more than 355 days. Every three years, it more or less catches up with the rest of the world through the addition of an extra month.

These 13-moon years are regarded as malevolent, and this provides a basis for the calendar's astrological use as a forecaster of cataclysm. Through the centuries, the wise men used the calendar to record the dates of tragedies, and in this way learned that there was only one way to avoid them – buffalo sacrifice. Throughout Batak country, the large number of buffalo horns decorating houses testifies to the depredation suffered by the poor beast in the name of devotion. The horns are a symbol of a man's wealth, and his capacity to prevail over adversity.

The Batak's religion was a secret known only to themselves when Christian missionaries appeared. Realising that the Batak would not abandon their cults, their calendar, their sacrifices and their spiritual dances, the missionaries accepted the frightening sculptures, but they added a cross, and they blessed the buffalo before sacrifice. The Batak took to some of the Christian ways, building themselves enormous monumental mausoleums decorated with a mixture of Christian and animist symbols.

All might now be well, but for the encroachment of tourism and the almighty dollar. It took less than 20 years to undo what Arab traders and Chinese merchants, Portuguese and Dutch colonisers, and Japanese invaders had failed to pull apart. The Toba Batak traded their heritage for small change and formica table-tops. Ancient calendars, masks, head-dresses, weapons, carvings, down to the very pillars of their houses, disappeared forever in the luggage of Western antique hunters, or reappeared in the tourist shops of Prapat.

Only now have the Batak started to regret, and to ponder. What is there to show, when everything has been sold, and hardly anyone knows how to make traditional objects any more? How can a person find peace in a village overrun by tourists, or in a house in which corrugated iron has replaced the great thatched roof, making it impossible to think through the din when it rains?

The Toba Bataks are at the most delicate crossroads of their long history. Will they find their identity again?

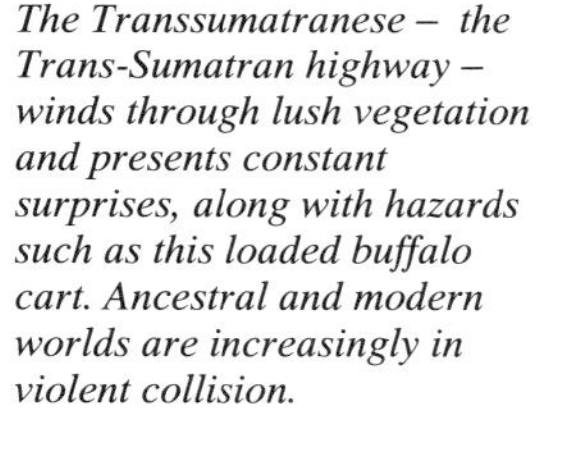

The Transsumatranese – the Trans-Sumatran highway – winds through lush vegetation and presents constant surprises, along with hazards such as this loaded buffalo cart. Ancestral and modern worlds are increasingly in violent collision.

Bali: Garden of the Gods

The crew of the first Western ship to reach Bali in the 16th century refused to leave. Word nevertheless got out, and Western artists flocking here in the 1930s portrayed a paradise of mankind's lost innocence – an image that Hollywood movies fixed and cheapened in gaudy colour.

It was a big burden for so small an island. The most immediate manifestation of innocence was soon expunged by the bureaucrats in Jakarta, who advised the bare-breasted Balinese to cover up (though the Dutch long before had begun the process – to protect their soldiers' morals, it was said). In 1963, the most sacred of Bali's volcanoes exploded and rained death upon paradise, and two years later Bali was the scene of some of the worst killing when anti-Communist hysteria turned all of Indonesia into a charnel house. Then came the jumbo jet and the tourist boom. It has been a lot to bear, but the people are resilient, and so is their culture.

More temples than homes

Bali is a gem of nature, the prize jewel in the world's most enchanting necklace of islands. An east-west parade of volcanoes reaches through the clouds and plunges into deep ravines mantled in green – high forests of pine, cypress and tall fern, and dense jungle down below. The drop is precipitous to the north, but centuries of artistry have carved the southern slopes into an exquisitely delicate pattern of *sawah* – intricately irrigated rice paddies that trip and twirl, down and around each contour, in a manner so perfect as to appear natural; this pictorial poem is punctuated by coconut groves, temples and tropical orchards. The volcanic soil is marvellously fertile, and combines with the short, violent monsoon downpours from October to May to assure abundant harvests.

Ancient belief holds Bali to be at the centre of the universe, riding the ocean on the back of a giant turtle. Another legend credits a great Hindu priest with cutting Bali free from Java – using his fingers as scissors. The original Balinese arrived from central Java as Islam spread there, and took over the island from the aboriginal Balinese. The shallow channel between Java and Bali is hardly a mile wide, but it was enough to save Bali for Hinduism; this is the only Indonesian island that Islam did not penetrate. On Bali, Javanese Hinduism fused with the islanders' existing animist faith to create an extraordinarily rich and complex set of beliefs and ritual observances.

Pura Besakih – the 'mother temple' of Bali – has shrines dedicated to each of the island's many gods, and is the scene of purification rites in which the entire population participates. Temporary altars have then to be constructed to take the piles of offerings. Pilgrims dress in white, and shrines are decked out in the colours of important gods.

The Balinese were left alone to develop their elaborate and sophisticated culture through several centuries of isolation, before being thrust rudely into the modern world by the conquering Dutch. In 1906, the flower of the Balinese aristocracy died dressed in all their finery: brandishing golden *krises,* they threw themselves against the Dutch guns in suicidal waves known as *puputan*.

The Besakih temple complex consists of about 50 component temples on seven stepped terraces 3000 feet up the side of Gunung Agung. It dates back at least 1000 years and was doubtless originally the site of sacrifices to the sacred volcano. Gunung Agung erupted in 1963, wiping out high villages, devastating crops, and covering all of Bali in a layer of volcanic ash, but miraculously, Besakih and its distinctive black pagodas were spared.

The surviving princes were stripped of their power and their tiny feudal kingdoms were disbanded, but the culture stayed intact, and the aristocratic remnants found a new role as patrons of the arts and guardians of the temples. Bali has been called the Land of a Thousand Temples, but this is a gross understatement. There are more than 5000 main temples, and since every home has a family temple, it can be said that Bali has more temples than it has homes.

The Balinese believe they are holding their island in trust for the gods. With so many gods, it adds up to a lot of responsibility. The Balinese worship the gods of Hindu India, but more real to them is a host of local gods, spirits and demons. There is a supreme deity with three manifestations – a god of creation, a god of protection and a god of destruction.

It all comes together at Pura Besakih, the island's holiest sanctuary, which lies on the slopes of the over 10,000-foot Gunung Agung, the highest and holiest of the island's mountains. Here, absolutely every god is honoured and worshipped, and once in every Balinese century it is the site of the *Eka Dasa Rundra*, a truly epic three-month round of ritual and animal sacrifices intended to purify the entire universe and to set it all to rights.

The Balinese had fallen behind in its observance when they scheduled 1963 as an *Eka Dasa Rundra* year. On March 17, Mount Agung erupted, killing 2000 people and laying waste large areas of the island. This demonstration of the wrath of the gods was taken to heart, and matters were put right with six months of ceremonies in 1979.

Morsels for the bad spirits, incense for the good

Religious observance is highly directional in Bali. The east is propitious as the abode of the sun god Surya. It is considered no coincidence that Mount Agung is in the east of the island, and the south-east is where most of Bali's 2.5 million people live. Mount Agung is the vortex of existence, and everything from ritual to architecture is given its own polarity: *kaja* (towards the mountain) or *kelod* (towards the sea). It is better to sleep with your head in a *kaja* direction, and to eat facing east. A farmer will transplant his rice seedlings with an eye on their *kaja-kelod* axis. Good spirits dwell in the mountains, while monsters and bad spirits live in the sea, and malevolent demons lurk on lonely beaches. The sea is suspect. Balinese bathe at least twice a day, regardless of whether it is spring water or from the gutter, but few know how to swim, or care to. The island fishing fleet is small.

The important thing is to keep all of the spirits content. You can do this by paying constant respect to the good spirits, while trying at the same time to mollify the bad ones with little offerings casually cast on the ground. You also do it by keeping the gods suitably entertained. Bali has been described as a 'theatre state', so bound up in drama and dance is everyday life. The Balinese have no word for 'art', for artistic expression and religious expression are for them one and the same thing: it is satisfying; it is fun and it makes life meaningful.

All Balinese take it for granted that they are artists of one kind or another. Sculptures, like shrines, are everywhere – stone guardians with monstrous faces,

The giant, droopy-branched waringin *– the banyan tree of India – graces sacred sites and may itself be used as a shrine upon which to deposit offerings. The god of the* waringin *stars in Balinese dance as the* barong, *a hairy creature who vanquishes the wicked witch Rangda.*

The Balinese love to bathe, and even speak of their faith as agama tirta *– the religion of the waters. Too often they regard water as a purifier and cleanser regardless of its condition; and pollution and water-borne disease are problems in areas where the same water source may be used for bathing, drinking, cooking and waste disposal.*

winged wooden lions, *garuda* eagle warriors. Worms eat away the wood and lichens eat into the soft volcanic stone, but decay is a part of life, and there is constant re-creation. The young mimic their parents, and in that way learn the intricacies of cutting out palm leaves, or crafting offerings. Gongs ring everywhere, and when the *gamelan* rehearses, the children come to sit and learn on the laps of the musicians, or they mimic the temple dances while their parents correct the position of head, hands and knees. Temple festivals are as much social as religious occasions. Cockfights provide excitement, an excuse for gambling, and a blood sacrifice to keep evil spirits at bay. Outside the temple there is all the fun of the fair. Inside, the dances are offerings delivered in clouds of incense.

Even the smallest village requires three temples for community life to function properly: the *Pura Puseh* (umbilical temple) at the *kaja* end of the village honours its founders; the *Pura Desa* (village temple) is concerned with the everyday needs of the living; the *Pura Dalem* (deep temple, or temple of the dead) is near the cemetery and cremation site, at the *kelod* end. Each temple has its own calendar of events to add to those of the district, and to the schedule of island-wide festivals; 'what is the rule in one village is the exception in the next,' noted a 1930s book on Bali.

These banana leaves are being turned into serving plates for offerings or ritual meals. The leaf is cut up, and the pieces pinned together with bamboo splinters. Older women make the best tukan banten *– offering makers. The woman here is dressed in her best batik sarong with a silk top and gold jewellery; the white head band a further expression of devotion.*

These edible towers (gebogan) *will be carried to the local temple on the heads of the women. The core of a* gebogan *is a length of bamboo spiked with sticks. Fruits, flowers and coloured rice cakes are attached; it is then garlanded with young coconut leaves. The divinities are content just to admire the offerings, and the towers will then be brought back home to be consumed.*

Balinese society is intensely communal, with each person bound from birth by a complex web of commitments to family, clan, caste and village. Each community is sub-divided into *banjars*, which do most of the social organising. Each has its *bale banjar* – a pavilion-like meeting place with a drum tower to summon members. Society is further stratified according to caste-like classes, although these are not as closed as those of Hindu India; nobody is untouchable, for example.

About 10 per cent belong to the three tiers of nobility – *Brahmana*, *Satrya* and *Waisy* – based upon lineages traced back to 14th-century Javanese rulers of the island. The Balinese language, like Javanese, also takes three forms: Low, Middle and High, each with variations in its style and vocabulary. Low is the most abrupt; Middle is rather more polite and High the most ornate; aristocratic High Balinese is still heard in daily use in East Bali, once the site of the island's most powerful kingdoms.

The ritual of rice

Rice growing is so important that it merits a special organisation, the *subak*, to ensure the equitable distribution of seed and water, to direct maintenance of the canal system and to intercede with the gods. A shrine is placed near each important dam and sluice, and every village sabak has its own temple. Water brought from the crater lake of Mount Batur (ranked second to Agung in the volcanic pantheon) will be used in rituals that mirror those of the rest of Balinese life. Rice grown on wet paddies (*sawah*) is the staple food, and Bali's rice growers can fairly claim to be among the world's best.

The *sawah* yield two crops a year. First the stalks of the previous harvest are burned off, then the field is ploughed dry, soaked with water, and ploughed and stamped to the consistency of glue. Seedlings are raised in a nursery patch, and after due ceremony, they are replanted, shoot by shoot, in rows a hand's width apart. The moment they take root, the water level has to be raised; it is a delicate stage, with great care taken to prevent the growth of choking algae. After three months, the crop receives offerings similar to those made to a pregnant woman, and when it is almost ripe, the paddy is drained. Little white-and-blue flags on bamboo canes flap in the wind, and children scamper about ringing bells to keep the birds and rats at bay.

Astral wheels and birds cavort above a crown of woven coconut leaves in this offering – a delicately crafted vision of the Balinese cosmos.

Men did the planting, but everyone helps in the harvest. The rice is taken to the village and dried on mats, after which it is husked. This is a joyful time, though storing the harvested grain in the rice barn calls for respect, and all joking is put aside lest it give offence to the spirits.

Should the yield drop, the paddy is switched to 'dry' crops – maize and sweet potatoes – and then refreshed with a dosage of ash and rotten vegetables. Rice is never the only crop. Eels dig their nests in the paddy walls, and are caught for the pot by night with the aid of a torch and bamboo stave. The *sawah* also harbours a duckpond that doubles as a fish farm: stocked at planting time, it gives up a harvest of full-grown fish when the paddy is dried. Other delicacies include *kaku*, dark green water snails that are delicious when boiled, dragonflies that make a high-protein grill, and various aquatic larvae that give the subtle aroma of seafood to the farmer's soups...

Grass roots provide the only reinforcement in this intricate system of dykes which demarcate the rice paddies above the Petanu River in the heart of Bali. The Petanu is a holy river, and springs near here are believed to have magical powers.

From the cry of the cockerel...

The traditional Balinese home recalls an ancient Roman villa, as it consists essentially of a large courtyard enclosed in white-washed walls, which protect it equally from prying eyes and disruptive demons.

For all their community spirit, the Balinese like some domestic privacy. A vegetable garden and orchard line the inside wall, and the family temple occupies a corner facing Mount Agung. Across the courtyard, behind a small retaining wall, is the pig pen. The kitchen is a smoky shack facing south. In the middle, among the hibiscus, are the *bale*, airy pavilions where the family sleep. The Balinese bed is a rigid mat raised about 3 feet off the ground. The Balinese plate is simplicity itself – a banana leaf, which will duly enrich the compost heap when discarded – and the hand is considered more sensitive and less barbaric than a spoon or fork.

The Bali day begins before dawn, when the first cockerel lets fly with a battle cry that is taken up from one end of the island to the other. After a quick breakfast of powdered peanuts and *tipak* – consisting of sticky steamed rice in a palm leaf – the father leaves for the rice paddy, a forked spade over his shoulder and a machete thrust into his sarong. His wife, meanwhile, prepares the main meal of the day, a pound of rice per person and a stew of meat chunks, vegetables and unripened papaya, cooked in coconut oil and sprinkled with grilled sliced shallots and peanuts, coarse salt and raw pimento. She heats the water that the rice was

washed in, adds left-over scraps, and takes it to the pigs, who come running when she calls: '*Bankung! ci ci ci tacita kung!*'

The little girls sweep the steps with a bamboo broom; they then balance earthen jugs on their heads and go to the spring for water. The boys stoke the cooking fires with dried coconut shell from the heap kept in the corner of the courtyard, and have fun chasing the dogs.

Barely awake, the grandparents take their first betel chew. The grandmother undoes her long, still-black hair, rearranges the sarong that sheathes her from waist to ankle, and joins her daughter-in-law in the kitchen. An expert in offerings, she takes portions of food and places them on small squares of banana leaf, then sets them down in the places she knows are favoured by demons – near the hearth, on the lowest step of each pavilion, by the entrance, on a bicycle seat ... and so on. The dogs may steal what the demons decline, which explains why some people suspect that they are in league.The heavenly spirits now receive due attention. The grandmother fashions a plate out of plaited palm leaf, and places on it a mini-chew of betelnut, together with red, yellow and white flowers – the colours of the gods. She carries this to the family temple, together with a smoking incense stick; with a practised flick of the wrist, she sends to heaven the fragrance that so pleases the deities.

Meanwhile, the grandfather has gathered the ducks and disappeared into the morning mist, guiding the flock towards the pond (*continued on p.135*)

The Balinese rice barn (lumbung) *is designed to protect the grain from insects, rats, and rot. A large wooden disc fitted to each support post foils the rodents. The storage space is reached by a small wooden door, often guarded by the figure of a bat or cat. The thick thatch provides welcome shade, and the wooden platform is covered with matting.*

The rice is high and harvesting has begun in this paddy. The rattan basket is topped by a sieve for sifting the grain.

A Balinese temple festival

First come the offerings of food, fruit and flowers, received by assistants dressed in white, and fussed over by the old women. The sound of the priest's bell mingles with the general clamour and the rhythms of the tireless temple musicians.

An open-air theatre has been erected in the temple forecourt. The bamboo stage is decorated with palm leaves; the footlights are kerosene lamps, and a set of brightly coloured curtains hides the backstage dressing area. All around, *warungs* selling rice dishes and *soto ayam* (chicken soup), and stalls offering trinkets, batik and toys are set up. These are served by young girls who wait nervously on customers under the amused eye of their mothers. In addition, there are buskers and *bakun* medicine men, card-sharps and cockfighting. Inside the temple, meanwhile, the priests chant encouragement to the gods to descend and enjoy the fun, and sometimes the thrones or images of the deities will be carried down to the river to receive a ritual bath.

After a communal dinner, the actors and dancers disappear behind the curtains into a chaos of make-up cases, costumes and masks. Dressers help with the make-up; coffee, tea, cakes, cigarettes are passed around; and children peep through the curtains at all the various mysteries within. There is no written script and no musical score, for the tales are well-known. The eldest and most experienced performer coaches the others in their big lines while chewing casually on betelnut.

The musicians of the village *gamelan* settle behind their instruments and, at a signal from behind the stage, they strike into a vibrant overture; they then set the tempo for the opening dance. An eye appears from behind the curtain, a quivering hand, a face frozen into a reincarnation of all the faces that have pleased god and villager down the ages. The entertainment will last through the night almost until dawn, when the gods are politely asked to take their leave, so that the people can go home.

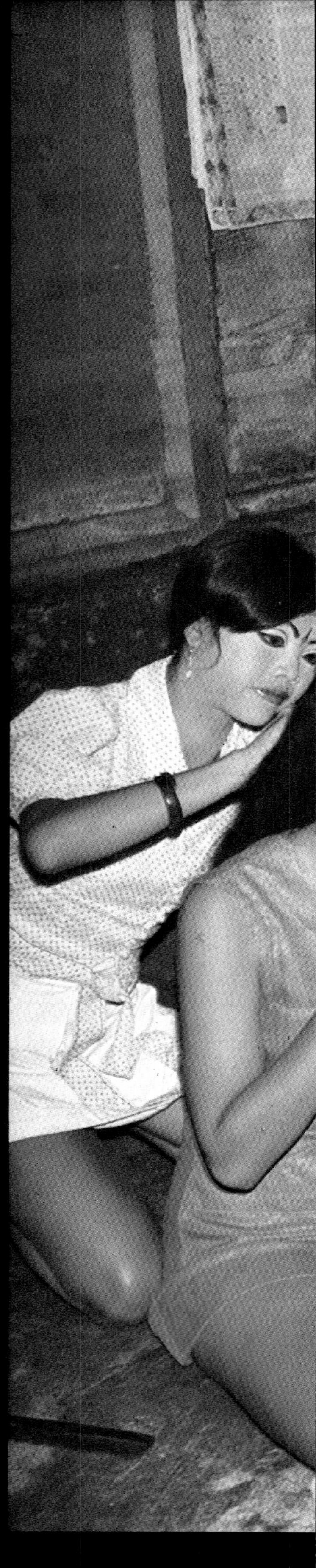

A legong *dancer is required to move with extraordinary agility and grace, despite being tightly sheathed in glittering gold brocade and having to contend with an elaborate headdress decorated with frangipanis. The* legong *originated as a court dance. It is peformed by two girls dancing in unison, and an attendant known as a* condong. *Balinese dancing is darting and cat-like, and charged with much more energy than its slow, sinuous Javanese counterpart.*

with a rooster feather dangling from the end of a cane. The children go to school wearing immaculate white shirts and shorts or beige skirts. They will be back by the end of the morning.

The women start for market, balancing baskets filled with bananas or papayas on their heads. Sometimes they haul a black pig on a leash, its back curved and stomach dragging. Ever since the government began to levy a tax on pig sacrifices (to limit the feast-day carnage), people are happy to sell one every now and then. It was worse during the Japanese occupation, when they had to go into hiding in order to sacrifice even a chicken.

A market is held every morning in the village, and twice a week in the district capital. The women take the *bemo* (minibus), which has room for 10 but carries 20; they pile aboard with animals and baskets. The market is awash with colours and odours: *jambu* fruit with its translucent flesh, and the *jeruk*, green and big as a football. Vegetables include the *bayem*, a kind of spinach, the *ketela*, sweet potato, the green papaya that will simmer with the meat. The *jaka palm* sugar bread is enticing, and the aroma of shrimp brine is so good that it makes one go weak at the knees...

It is also a market for news, and gossip is exchanged as fast as the sticky currency; the market woman rolls and threads the banknotes into the earlobe that once, on her wedding day, contained leaves of purest gold. For

Balinese dance consists in the main of a series of postures (agem) *connected by quick, high-stepping movements, and dramatic facial expressions. The basic stance is that of classic India, with legs turned out, knees bent, head tilted and hands providing most of the expression. The dancer depicted here is performing the* condong *role in the* legong *dance.*

Balinese dancing continues to evolve, much as ballet does in the West. The island's most popular tourist spectacle is the kecak, *a modern adaptation of a trance dance in which young girls swayed in time to a chanted chorus until they became possessed and were carried round the village to cast out disease.*

A kecak *is mesmerising when performed by a circle of up to 100 men wearing chequered loin cloths. They sway in unison and flutter their fingers as their 'Kechakachakachaka' chant mounts to a crescendo. This chant, however, is merely the accompaniment to actors performing a type of traditional play.*

Like the dancing that it accompanies, Balinese gamelan *music is much livelier and sharper-toned than the measured rhythms of Java. The variety of the orchestras is enormous. Among the most popular is the gong* kebyar, *with up to 30 players on gongs, metallophones, cymbals and bamboo flutes, and a pair of drummers setting complex, interlocking rhythms. Here a four-man* reong *provides a background syncopation.*

those with insufficient time, ready-made offerings are on sale so that thanks can be discharged at the market temple.

...to the fall of night

Around 11am, the women or children bring meals to the men resting in the shade of an awning on the edge of the rice paddy. *Tengga hai*, midday, is not a time to move about, and everyone who can heads for home.

Afternoon is for chores. The mother grates dried coconut into a basin. The grandfather has gone to the forest to cut bamboo and to help his son repair a house frame. A little girl, her younger brother on her hip, goes to a neighbour to return a bag of coffee borrowed the day before. The boys construct a gigantic kite, draw or listen to Radio Bali on a transistor set. The grandmother spins cotton on an old loom. Grandfather and ducks return from the paddy. Clambering aboard the beast's large back, the grandson returns the rented buffalo. Men and women go to bathe in the river in separate groups, men upstream, women downstream.

Back from the river, the women gather on the steps, while the father releases his prize fighting cock from its cage, massages it, polishes its beak, examines the eyes and the lustrous comb. The young children watch everything with big serious eyes. Everyone trails to the kitchen to get a cold meal, and each eats in a corner, silently. Eating, unlike bathing, is not conducive to chatter. But afterwards, the women relax, the head of one on the knees of another.

Sudden nightfall – *sanya kala* – seldom catches the Balinese out of doors. Night belongs to thinkers, artists and talkers. In clean shirt and smart sarong, they visit one another, or sit under the *bali bandjar,* or at a table of the *warung*, the open-air cafe that doubles as a grocery, where they drink *tuak* (palm wine) and eat sweets. The sculptors and painters finish their day's work by the light of the kerosene lamp.

To live fully, and die dreaming

Religious rites guide a Balinese from before birth until long after death. They begin in the third month of pregnancy, with offerings at the family temple and at a spring or river. Once born, the baby may not touch the ground for over a month, and so is carried everywhere. Children are privileged beings in Bali, since it is believed that the younger the person, the purer the soul. At 210 days – the Bali calendar year – offerings are made for the child, thus commencing a life-long cycle of rituals, through puberty, marriage, parenthood and death. One of the most onerous occurs at adolescence, when prominent teeth are filed down, lest the youth be taken for a demon. A girl at puberty is carried from her home in cloth robes patterned in gold leaf, with gold earrings and a golden crown of flowers. The priest sprinkles her with holy water and flower petals, and water is sprinkled through a mat (as in the marriage ceremony) into her cupped palms; she drinks the water and touches her hands to her forehead. She is purified, and a woman.

Cremation is not always sufficient to guarantee transit of the soul, so families organise an encore as double indemnity. Effigies are placed on plates of hammered silver and taken in procession to be burned. The ashes are then scattered on the sea. This procession is near Gianyar, home of Bali's weaving industry. The coloured sashes of the women are required wear in temple worship.

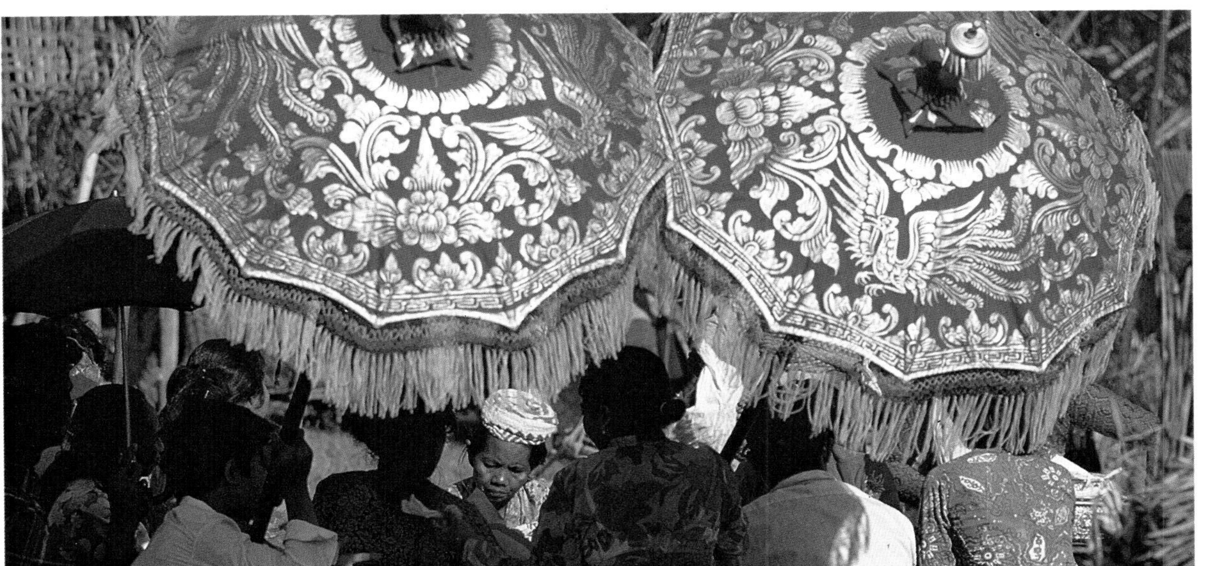

There is no telling what a procession winding through Bali's lush countryside might portend. Here Rangda the witch goddess is enjoying a jaunt around the village.

Parasols confer a celestial grace upon the activities which they shield from the sun. No ceremony is complete without these aristocratic accessories.

Marriage is essential if a person is to take the proper place in adult society, and the Balinese code is ingenious in ensuring that relations between men and women achieve this end. There is even an appropriate ritual for the *ngerorod* marriage by kidnapping. Families sometimes employ this device, in order to get round any caste problems.

A man needs a son, for only a son is properly qualified to take charge of the funeral ceremonies which will allow the father's soul to depart without remorse. In Bali, there are countless codified ways to do things, even dying... there is, for example, the pleasant method known as *mimpi* – while dreaming. Death holds no fear for the Balinese, since it is merely a pause before rebirth and eventual *moksa*: release through unity with the supreme spirit. Ideally, a person is cremated as soon as possible, but Balinese-style cremation is costly, and sometimes a body is buried while funds are raised, or until some rich relative dies and a piggy-back deal can be arranged.

Cremation preparations, especially in the case of a noble, are long and costly in materials and labour. First, the body is laid out in the family courtyard, in a temporary coffin decorated with flowers and bright ornaments. A fanciful pagoda-like tower with protective demon masks is constructed, as much as 60 feet high and resting on a base in the shape of a turtle entwined by sacred snakes. The body is bound in cloth inscribed with sacred texts; on an auspicious date determined by priestly divination, it is placed on top of the turtle – thereby symbolically suspended between heaven and earth.

The huge structure is carried through the streets by scores of men, who form a zig-zag procession followed by a *gamelan* (mainly percussion) orchestra, by crowds of relatives and friends, bearers of food, flowers and other offerings, and by a large wooden image of a bull, carved in a style reminiscent of ancient Egypt. The tower is regularly rotated to excited cries, until, almost toppling, it resumes its progress. This manoeuvre disorientates the soul, discouraging it from having second thoughts and trying to find its way back home. The procession wheels three times around the burning-place; the body is then removed from the tower and placed inside the hollow body of the bull, which is bound with bright ribbon strung with paper decorations. Then all is set alight, usually with a magnifying glass trained on the sun.

In a few minutes, 20 million rupees and months of work will have gone up in smoke. It is the eldest son's duty to stir the debris and to check that the body has been fully consumed. A few days later a colourful procession sets off for the sea (or the nearest river if the sea is too far away) to scatter the ashes on the cleansing waters.

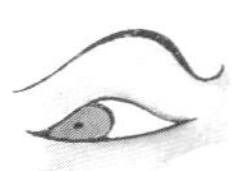

A noble is cremated in Ubud, the southern upland town that is the artistic and cultural centre of Bali. Family members will collect the ashes and wrap them in white linen with flowers and old Chinese coins; they will then be scattered over the sea.

The eyes are the mirrors of the soul and, as a result, the artistic styles that emphasise their form are strictly codified. Here, from left to right, are a woman, a man and a devil.

Sulawesi: Buffalo Heaven and Hell

The man moves slowly into the centre of a circle formed by all the inhabitants of the village. He has the piercing look of someone charged with a capital mission that he is on the point of accomplishing. He leads an enormous white buffalo towards the village headman. The docile animal follows.

Upon a barely perceptible signal from the headman, the man with the buffalo tugs gently on the lead connected to a ring in the beast's nostril. A machete swings, and a single unbelievably powerful blow severs the buffalo's neck artery. Blood gushes from the gaping wound and children rush forward with hollow bamboos to catch the crimson, bubbling liquid. The buffalo totters for a moment or two, and then drops heavily to the ground.

The mountain people of Sulawesi believe that the soul of a buffalo provides transport for the soul of a dead man on the long road to the afterworld. The critical moment of the *mabadong* – the Toraja funeral rite – has passed successfully, and the crowd rejoices. Bring on another buffalo...

The old spice route

Sulawesi looks like a wrecked starfish drifting between the islands of Borneo and New Guinea. Its old name was the Celebes, from the Portuguese word for 'infamous': they lost several ships on the reefs off its huge 3000-mile coastline and took it to be a cluster of islands, since they could not credit that so many points of land separated by great stretches of water were all joined together. The Spanish followed the Portuguese, then came the Dutch, English, French, and even the Danish, all of them wanting to control the lucrative spice trade that centred on the sultanates in the

The share-out of buffalo meat after a funeral sacrifice is no simple matter. Each mourner is entitled to a piece, selected on the basis of rank and relationship. This can lead to disputes which, if not quickly resolved, can end in violence.

southern part of the island. The Dutch eventually prevailed in 1669, after dispatching a large fleet from their base at Batavia (modern Jakarta) to subdue the powerful Sultan of Gowa who ruled much of the south of the island, but resistance by the proud and industrious Bugis and Macassarese people continued right into the 20th century.

Gowa became Macassar under the Dutch – famous for the perfumed hair oil that bore its name and without which no 19th-century dandy felt properly dressed. Now it is Ujung Pandang, the administrative and business capital of Sulawesi: a clamorous city of honking traffic, modern supermarkets, abject beggars and old Dutch canals that are now used as refuse dumps. Yet the Bugis still set sail from one of its three harbours in their schooners, trading to all corners of Indonesia and beyond.

The Bugis are the great sailors of the East. Still fiercely independent, they have the reputation of being the most *kasar* (tough and abrasive) of Indonesia's people, and they are certainly among its most enterprising. In earliest times they are thought to have roved an arc from Australia as far west as Madagascar. Today, they run what must be the largest remaining sailing fleet in the world, and apart from a certain unfortunate propensity to prey on pleasure craft and Vietnamese refugee boats, they perform an important transportation role, carrying goods and navigating the labyrinth of the archipelago without need of compass, map or radio.

The wide-beamed *prahu* is built of teak to a centuries-old design that the Bugis orginally copied from the Dutch; no metal or nails are used, only wooden pegs, and the Bugis shipwright needs no

The clove plant looks insignificant, but desire for its precious spice was what sparked the age of European exploration and conquest. The Indonesians even put cloves in their cigarettes.

The black pig is second only to the buffalo as a ceremonial sacrifice. Pigs can reach well over 600 lbs, at which stage they can hardly move.

blueprints. *Praha* appear clumsy to handle, but in fact, they are fast and manoeuvrable even when loaded to the deck with cargo; sometimes there is a tendency to overload, and a dozen have been known to go down in a single stormy night.

Sulawesi is a natural fortress, or rather four fortresses, since each arm is isolated from the others by jungled ravines and high peaks, with a few deep lakes (*danau*) gouged out between – the deepest, Matana, reaching down nearly 2000 feet. Several exotic species have found sanctuary in its steamy nooks and crannies. Creatures unique to Sulawesi include the tusked pig-deer *(bairusa),* a dwarf buffalo *(anoa)* no more than three feet tall, the saucer-eyed *tarsier,* and the *maleo* bird, which seems to think it is a reptile and buries its eggs in warm sand. There is also the Celebes black-crested ape, with a tiny stump tail and hairless black face, which the people of some local tribes, even without the help of Darwin's theory of evolution, regarded as their ancestor.

In addition to all these, Sulawesi also has 9 million human inhabitants speaking a confusing medley of some 50 different languages. As well as the Bugis and Macassarese, there are the nomadic, jungle-dwelling Toala, the light-skinned Gorontalese from the west and north, and the Minahassen who live in and around the island's second city of Manado in the far north-east. The Minahassen are a tall, sturdy race with light skins and high noses, whose life style is the most westernised of the island's peoples; unlike the Muslim Bugis and others, most are Christians, and live in well-ordered villages and towns.

For originality and idiosyncrasy, however, even the *maleo* bird has to give pride of place to the Toraja, the 'Men of the Mountains'.

Men of the mountains

The Toraja received their name from the Bugis, who drove their ancestors into the interior after failing to convert these lovers of pork and palm wine to Islam. An

This Toraja rice barn is decorated with a care matched only by the treatment accorded its precious contents. A good barn is damp-proof, rat-proof, insect-proof and a status symbol besides.

airport planted in their midst means that the Toraja are nowadays subject to instant invasion by plane-loads of German, French and Japanese tourists. But to appreciate properly the fortress quality of *Tana Toraja* – Torajaland – hardy travellers need to attempt the journey along the road that was constructed into the region in the late 1970s.

The coast north from Ujung Pandang consists of long stretches of beach dotted with fishing villages and backed by a wall of mountain all smothered in impenetrable jungle. The road attacks the mountain head-on, crawling laboriously up canyons overhung by towering peaks. Great trees with tentacled branches grab and lean over a fatal drop to the dizzy depths opening up below. Here is the kingdom of the monstrous 30-foot python, the 6-inch spider, and the 4-inch cockroach; there are also giant butterflies that will alight on your hand.

Wonderfully carved buffalo-head cornices are to be found in the village of Kele Kesu. The horns record the number of buffaloes killed by the family during acts of worship.

The Toraja rice barn is modelled on the dwelling. The number, and extent of their decoration, determines the wealth of a village. Neighbours are encouraged to sit on the porch between the pillars, the better to appreciate the weight of harvest suspended above them.

A Toraja house is more than just a home: it is a source of intense family pride, and one of the most beautiful craft constructions in the world. The fantastic roof is composed of superimposed layers of bamboo, split lengthwise and lashed together in a manner that combines strength with equilibrium and extraordinary lightness of aspect.

After a few hours, the landscape softens and the road descends into a widening upland valley. Before the Dutch conquered them and sent in Calvinist missionaries early in the 20th century, the Toraja were head-hunters living in fortified villages on the summits of their rocky hills. The Dutch ordered them down.

Nobody knows where the Toraja originated, and their own accounts of their history vary. One tradition has it that they voyaged to Sulawesi by canoe from somewhere to the south-west; another claims direct descent from the heavens, which was one reason they liked to place their villages as high as possible. Some see a clear maritime influence in the design of the Toraja house, or *tongkonan*, a magnificent structure raised on piles and topped with a monumental roof that rears up 40 to 50 feet at either end, rather like the bow and stern of a boat.

A grand elaboration of what the Batak and others do in Sumatra, it can equally be seen as representational of the head and horns of a buffalo. Since certain Toraja chants have a sea-going flavour, and the houses are festooned with buffalo images and horns, the issue remains open. A village never consists of more than half a dozen *tongkonan*, each of them home to a large extended family; all face north, which is consequently another direction from which the Toraja are supposed to have originated.

'Enlarge the circle and let all the mourners come...' Hundreds customarily respond to such an invitation to a mabodong *funeral rite.*

The procession has formed, and the coffin is about to be loaded aboard a hearse. The widow will join her husband for the ride...

The procession careers around the village, the atmosphere by now somewhat heated by the effects of palm wine. Hearse and deceased have all been severely shaken up. The funeral reaches its climax.

The buffalo hardly has time to collapse before the crowd rushes forward, driving sharpened bamboos into the gaping wound to gather the blood. Death, life and joy all come together at such a moment in Toraja country.

The missionaries made the Toraja at least nominal Christians by linking the teachings of Christ to the image of a favourite family god, *Puang Matua*. But, in fact, this hardly simplified matters, for Toraja theology is most complicated, with the journey of a person's soul to the afterworld being particularly arduous. Indeed, what really marks the Toraja as special is what happens when they die. Not since Tutankhamun has a people put such immense effort into preparing for the hereafter. The reason is much the same as it was in ancient Egypt. The Toraja believe that you can take it all with you. Meanwhile, for the relatives who have to stay behind and try to provide for their departed kinsman, the consequences can be ruinous.

Puya, the Toraja heaven, is a very status-conscious place, and the ancestors expect the dead to arrive in much the same economic shape that they enjoyed in life – otherwise, the ancestors may turn nasty. Moreover, heavenly expectations mount in relation to the deceased person's standing and affluence. A small child is welcome in heaven with the comparatively modest sacrifice of one little pig, but the souls of an entire herd of buffalo are the only fitting company for the soul of a really grand man.

In Torajaland, a person is not dead until buried, and in the case of an eminent person that can mean a long, long wait while all the necessary preparations are being made. In the meantime, the corpse is treated much as a sick person. Dressed in finely woven cloth, it is dutifully propped up in a sitting position, offered food, chatted to, and generally treated as if it were still one of the family.

The coffin is levered up to its last resting place in a vault carved out of a high cliff not far from the village. For years to come, the deceased will gaze down in effigy from an adjoining balcony.

The high price of heaven

The burial ceremonies can last several days, during which hundreds of guests arriving from far and wide have to be looked after and accommodated; usually a temporary village is erected. When everyone has assembled, a circle of 'those who cry' forms around the body, and the *mabadong* songs of praise and ritual dancing kick off the funeral proper.

Sometimes the coffin is paraded in joyous procession around several neighbouring villages, and there will be days of bullfighting, kick-boxing and similar entertainments, and nights of feasting and chanting. The climax of the whole round of festivities – the slaughter of as many as 50 animals – takes place with the celebrants in a state of collective delirium. The coffin is finally placed in a high mountain vault, and a life-like wooden effigy (*tau-tau*) is propped on a cliff ledge overlooking the valley.

The Indonesian government has tried to regulate sacrificial slaughter, officially to protect the herds, but also because there is a limit to what it will tolerate from the ethnic minorities. A heavy fine is levied on any village that slaughters too many animals, but this rarely prevents people from indulging in their ancestral rites. Instead, the fine only serves to increase the community's indebtedness.

In spite of all such restraining regulations, and the timid influence of Christianity, ancient tradition is the only value reference that these people have. For the Toraja, the sacrificial buffalo and pig are economic regulators. By feeding the poor, by spreading some of the wealth of the better-off and by enabling the successful to climb to a higher caste through grand disbursement, the slaughter ensures that Toraja society continues to evolve.

But when tradition threatens the equilibrium of a society, it becomes a danger. Nowadays, stock prices in Torajaland have become exhorbitant; an albino animal costs as much as a car does in the West, an adult pig fetches as much as a moped. With their herds decimated, Toraja families go into debt for years, and as a result the whole fragile economy of the region is placed in jeopardy.

The Lesser Sundas: Isles of the Ancestral Spirits

Beyond Java and Bali, there stretches a constellation of small islands like stepping stones across a pond. They are the protruding peaks of submerged mountains, and mark the southern perimeter of the Indonesian archipelago. The Dutch sought to distinguish them from the 'Greater Sundas' – Java, Sumatra and Borneo – though properly they now have the Indonesian name of Nusa Tenggara, meaning the South-East Islands.

They include some of the most unstable places on earth. When Sumbawa had its last big convulsion in 1815, the volcano Tambora ejected so much debris into the atmosphere that it created a notorious 'year without summer' all over the world. Flores has 14 active volcanoes, plus a volcanic conundrum in the three lovely crater lakes of Keli Matu: each changes colour every few years. Between Flores and Sumbawa, on smaller islands isolated by swirling currents, lives the fearsome Komodo dragon, the world's largest lizard – and possible origin of the Chinese dragon myth. It can reach a length of 10 feet, and lives as long as 100 years. Despite its great bulk, it can be a nimble mover, especially when a prey is in sight ... including an occasional human being who rashly gets too close.

A mosaic of peoples

Over the millennia, the south-east islands have acted as a gigantic net to catch drifting shoals of human migration. Ethnologists are mired in theories about who came from where, and when: about 'Proto-Malaysians' and 'Deutro-Malaysians', Melanesian and Chinese, Negritoes and Aborigines, and who-knows-who-else besides who made landfalls here. A scattering of megaliths, for instance, and the continued ritual use of large stone slabs on Sumba, suggest links with prehistoric China. Islam swept through the islands in the 15th century; then came the Portuguese seeking sandalwood and souls, then the Dutch.

The whole process of upheaval, human as well as geological, still continues. Portuguese and Dutch fought to a draw over Timor, and divided up the island, the Portuguese taking the eastern half. As many as 50,000 East

Perhaps 20 whales a year are killed off Lambata Island by this spectacular method. The whale meat is shared out, with harpooner and boat-owner getting most. The blubber is turned into oil for lamps. The same two families have received the heads as traditional tribute for hundreds of years. When whales are scarce, sharks, dolphins or manta rays may be harpooned.

The traditional island home on stilts has added practicality on Komodo. The desolate interior of the island is prowled by the famous dragons: sharp-fanged, sharp-clawed lizards twice the size of a man and capable of gobbling a small goat whole.

The Sumba cooking hearth is sited in the middle of the multi-family dwelling between the four roof pillars. Spirit objects are placed in an overhead loft, and the spirits consulted at every turn.

Timorese were killed in the Second World War during fighting between the occupying Japanese and Australian forces, and possibly twice as many perished after the Indonesian army invaded in 1976 in order to snuff out an independence movement which arose when the Portuguese finally departed. At an appalling cost, including the relocation of up to 90 per cent of its native population, East Timor became the 27th province of Indonesia.

This is a transitional zone, known to naturalists as Wallacea, after Sir Alfred Russel Wallace, Darwin's rival, who spent years in these islands discovering how Eurasian and Australasian animal species merged. The climate is transitional too. Eastward along the island chain, it becomes drier as hot winds from the bone-dry heartlands of Australia push the moist monsoon towards South-East Asia during the middle part of the year.

Lombok is a case in point. It is separated from Bali by a deep strait, and blessed with its own holy volcano, Mount Rinjani, which at 12,225 feet is the highest mountain in the whole of Indonesia. It is also an island of stark physical and cultural contrasts. It has an abundant wildlife – including no fewer than eight different kinds of kingfisher, intriguing black and crimson flower peckers and golden orioles – and its rain forests are as lush as any on Bali, but it has parched areas as well. Occasional droughts can ruin the rice crop, as it did last in 1966, when 50,000 of the island's people died of starvation.

Lombok's 2 million people are a mix of local Sasak, Balinese, Chinese, Arabs, Javanese and Bugis, all of whom stick doggedly to their distinctive ways of life. The Muslim Sasak have somewhat edgy relations with the Hindu Balinese (who were for many centuries the Sasak's overlords), and are themselves split between orthodox followers of Islam and the highly unorthodox *Wektu-telu* of the mountains, who believe in Allah, in Mohammed as his prophet, and a lot else besides, including the power of the sun, moon, stars and ancestral spirits. Like other Muslims, they pray facing Mecca, but unlike the others never go there; they scorn mosques and enjoy pork, since it is clearly, they believe, a provision of Allah.

Mass tourism ends at the Lombok Strait – at least for now – and *orang bulan* (whites – literally 'moon persons') take on a rarity value which is evident in the trails of curious children who want to touch you. Ancient ways of *adat* – ritual custom – are closer to the surface here; Islam or Christianity are veneers overlaying deeper beliefs in ancestral and nature spirits. On Lombok, the saying goes that 'without *adat*, we are no more than the horse or cow'. *Adat* is the unwritten code of responsibilities that regulates a community's traditional way of doing everything, from before birth to beyond the grave.

The rules vary as much as any kind of dance or cultural display always does, but there are certain general patterns throughout the region: animal sacrifices, for example, and the feasts that they provide; and ritualised contests, usually involving a little symbolic blood-letting, to ensure good crops and fruitful marriages. Flores has its *caci*, when masked warriors lash one another with whips to the bang of

This Timor house is of a type favoured by aboriginal tribes on the forest fringe; these people practise subsistence farming (manioc, maize, copra) and provide cheap labour for the Indo-Malay majority population.

On Sumba, as everywhere in Indonesia, the traditional village is undergoing a transformation. Nowadays these distinctive conical thatched roofs are often replaced by corrugated iron. The hillside behind shows evidence of slash-and-burn agriculture. Forest that has been felled and then set on fire will produce a variety of crops, but the ash nutrients are soon used up and the minerals in the soil are dissolved and washed away.

gongs and drums. On Sumba, hundreds of mounted warriors wearing scarf-turbans participate in the *pasola*, a ritual battle involving violent cavalry charges. Not too long ago, the blood-letting was real.

Rosaries and skull-trees

Sumbawa Island is as devoutly Muslim as anywhere in Indonesia, with loudspeakers waking the faithful to 4am prayers, but even here *adat* is respected and the *dukun* or medicine man consulted.

Neighbouring Flores is devoutly Catholic, but in a way that accommodates the ancestral spirits. It used to be called Snake Island, because the ancestral spirits (*nitu*) who were believed to inhabit its rocks and rivers used pythons to warn people when danger threatened. In 1512, the Portuguese named it *Cabo das Flores*, Cape of Flowers, after the lush vegetation of its rich volcanic soils. They established missions as well as forts, and when power changed hands, Dutch Jesuits took over their evangelistic work, so that most of the 1 million Flores islanders are Catholic, and almost every village has its church.

Palm wine (tuak) *is the noble drink of non-Muslim islanders, and is served at all great occasions. Here the palm sap has just been pressed. It will remain in these jars for some time before fermention in bamboo containers. Stronger* arak *is produced by distilling the* tuak. *Another type of* arak *is distilled from rice wine, but is less in favour with Indonesians.*

These rice barns on Lombok are communally-owned and storage is communal, too, to maximise the speed and efficiency of harvesting. Each farmer's share will be determined by a complex calculation that takes account of the yield of his paddies and the time he has put into maintenance and other work.

The barn design reflects the influence of the island's rich and elegant neighbour Bali, whose princes ruled western Lombok for 200 years, and all of the island for much of the 19th century.

Sawu women perform a pedoa *fertility dance. Their ankle baskets are filled with seashells and act like castanets. Their sarongs are of* ikat *cloth, created by an immensely skilled and painstaking procedure in which the cotton threads are tie-dyed before being woven.* Ikat *is the high craft of the south-east islands. Once restricted to ceremonial wear, some* ikat *cloths used to take years to complete. There is an immense diversity of pattern and colour, with styles changing from village to village as well as from island to island. Sawu lies between Timor and Sumba. It has a matrilineal class system, divided between the* hubi ae *and* hubi iki, *which translates as larger and lesser flower-stalks.*

On Flores, Roman dogma and age-old animism entwine. The occasional sacrifice of a pig to the ancestors makes a Flores Catholic no less devout; and who is to say whether carvings of serpents with male and female figures recall the Garden of Eden, or the warnings of the *nitu*? The Flores town of Bajawa is the scene of an annual Mass that precedes a ritual deer hunt connected with puberty and fertility rites. After the Mass, swordsmen carry the holy cross through the town's streets. After the hunt, young girls dip their hands in the deer blood.

At the eastern tip of the island, where the Portuguese first established themselves, a fine Catholic cathedral graces the port of Larankuta, and women still say the rosary in Portuguese. Nevertheless, the many surviving pagan rites of the local Lamaholot people are an anthropologist's delight. For centuries, the Lamaholot were split into two groups who waged ritual combat, apparently as a way of producing human sacrifices to secure their mutual well-being.

Avowedly pagan practice has survived most on Sumba. In spite of the once-profuse forests of sandalwood that gave it its old name of Sandalwood Island, it was poor enough and remote enough to escape much attention – even if today's Australian surfers have begun to exploit another, unsuspected asset. As much as half of Sumba's half-million inhabitants still practise *marapu*, a spirit cult that puts a high price on death. Again there is deliberate destruction of wealth – typically, buffalo and horses – while more gruesome days are recalled by the 'skull-tree' motif woven into their brilliantly hued *ikat* cloth. Another custom to survive is polygamy – men from the island's ruling caste still like to have more than one wife at a time.

'One nation, one language...'

A shared experience of Dutch colonialism was all that Indonesians had in common when they won their independence in 1949. This problem of chronic diversity is nowhere more dramatically demonstrated than on Alor, a volcanic outcrop a couple of stepping-stones beyond Flores. Alor is 60 miles by 20 miles at its widest points, yet it is so rugged that its 100,000 people are splintered into 50 tribes speaking 50 languages. There are seven different language groups on Alor, and five on its tiny neighbour, Pantar. Heads were still being hunted 30 years ago, and telegraph wire was prized for the superior quality of arrowhead that could be manufactured from it.

The one thing that united the people of Alor was a passion for old bronze gongs known as *mŏko*, left scattered about the island by some long-forgotten people, and deemed essential in the acquisition of a quality bride. On Alor they still cherish *mokos*, but they no longer go to war over them. Thanks to the one-language pledge of 1949, and the spread of *Bahasa Indonesia*, even *moko* collectors can now get together to discuss their treasures.

The banyan, the sacred tree of Hindu and Buddhist alike, is found all over Indonesia, where it is known as the waringin. *Through the branches taking root, banyans can attain a circumference of 70 feet or more. A banyan grows at each corner of a Batak village in Sumatra, and it is often the centrepiece of a village in Bali.*

Gazetteer

Japan

The islands which make up Japan, or Nippon as it is officially known, occupy only a tiny area on the fringe of Asia. Yet the country is the third most powerful industrial nation in the world; it has been predicted that by the turn of the century Japan will outstrip even the United States in economic strength.

Japan's astonishing rise to the status of economic 'super-power' has been accomplished only in the last hundred years. Today the Japanese people – 80 per cent of whom live in towns and cities – enjoy an increasingly high standard of living, achieved by a combination of intense effort and sophisticated technology. They are governed within a democratic system which preserves, as a symbol of national unity, the oldest monarchy in the world.

The ancestors of the Japanese had probably arrived from mainland Asia by c. AD 100. In the 4th century AD the Japanese conquered a region at the tip of southern Korea, which they held for some 200 years. From or through Korea, new skills and customs were gradually adopted in Japan – two examples being rice cultivation and the Chinese method of writing.

From the middle of the 6th century, Buddhism, introduced from China through Korea, made much headway in Japan, where it won the support of the imperial family. Buddhism supplemented the existing Japanese religion, associated with

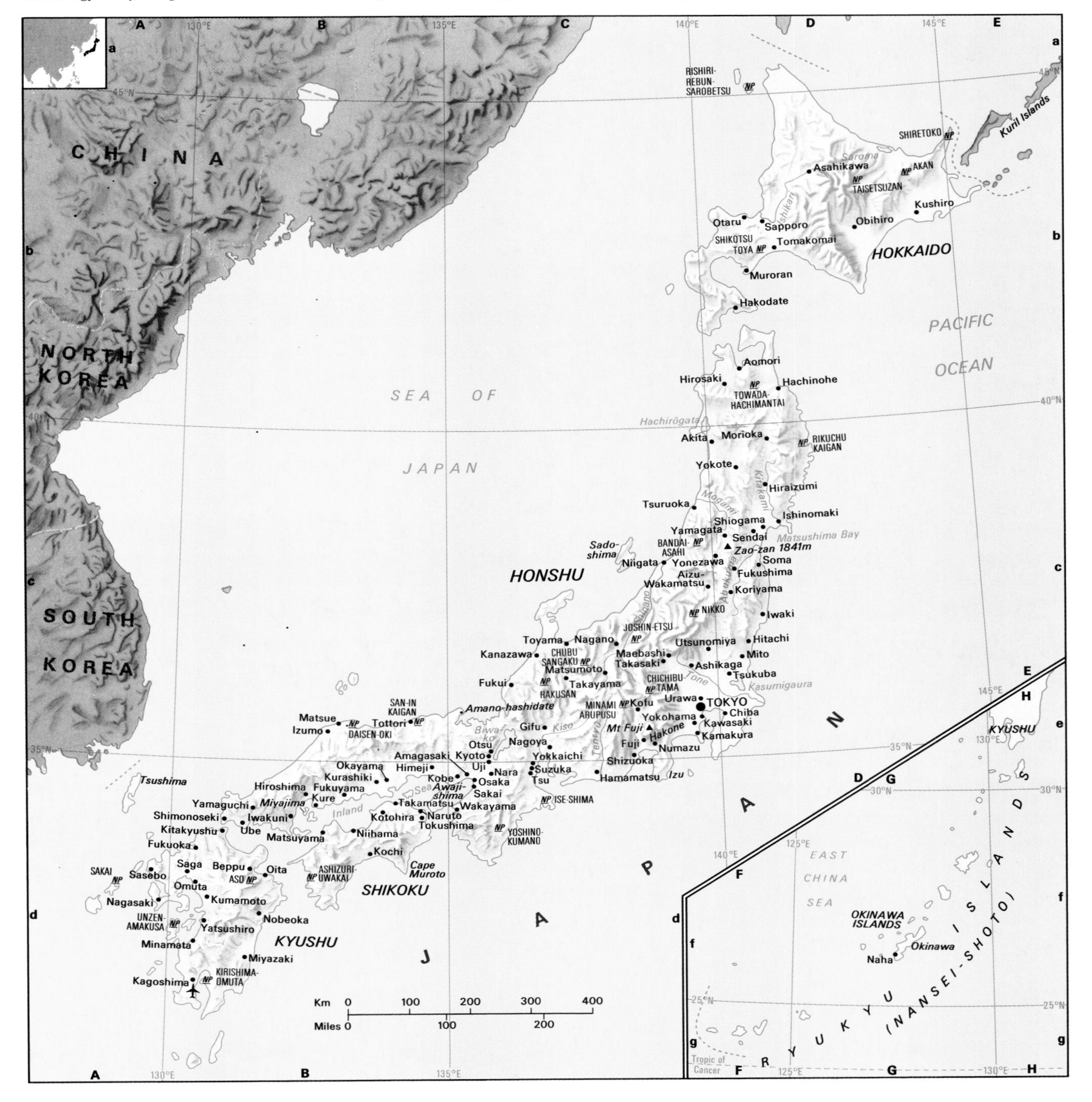

JAPAN AT A GLANCE
Area 143,750 square miles
Population 123,642,000
Capital Tokyo
Government Parliamentary monarchy
Currency Yen
Language Japanese
Religions Shinto (79%), Buddhist (81%), Christian (1%) (a majority is both Shinto and Buddhist)
Climate Temperate, monsoonal; average temperature in Tokyo ranges from -2 to 8°C (28-46°F) in January to 22-30°C (72-86°F) in August
Main primary products Rice, potatoes, sweet potatoes, tea, fruit, vegetables, edible seaweeds, timber, poultry, fish and shellfish; coal, sulphur
Major industries Iron and steel, nonferrous metals, ships, cars, motorcycles, electrical and electronic equipment, textiles, oil refining, petrochemicals, fertilisers, cement, optical goods, watches, fishing, food processing, forestry
Main exports Motor vehicles, machinery, electrical and electronic goods, iron and steel, chemicals, instruments, textiles, ships, metal goods
Annual income per head (US$) 9684
Population growth (per thous/yr) 4
Life expectancy (yrs) Male 76 **Female** 82

sun worship and known as Shinto ('The Way of the Gods').

In 710 a new capital was built at Nara on the contemporary Tang Chinese model, marking the heyday of early Buddhism in Japan. A large capital, Heian-kyo, also built on the Chinese pattern, was founded in 794. It was later to be called Kyoto. The Heian period lasted for almost four centuries; it is notable for two developments – the speedy growth of a distinctive Japanese culture among the aristocrats and the loss of effective political power by the emperor.

Yoritomo, the leader of a samurai group, became virtual ruler of Japan in 1185. Henceforth, the samurai, the fighting man, dominated Japanese society. The emperor granted Yoritomo the title of shogun, which is the abbreviation of a Japanese term meaning 'barbarian-suppressing generalissimo'.

Yoritomo's successors in the Kamakura shogunate lacked his ability, and effective power passed to the warrior household of Hojo. The Kamakura period saw the consolidation of warrior society, the growth of a Japanese form of Buddhism, known as Zen, the fine art of the swordsmith and the origin of seppuku *(suicide by disembowelment).*

The Kamakura were followed, in 1336, by the Ashikaga shogunate and a period marked by a series of civil wars between various warrior barons. From 1543 onwards, Portuguese traders began to arrive in Japan, soon followed by Catholic missionaries. In the early 17th century, the most powerful figure in Japan was Tokugawa Ieyasu, who defeated his rivals in 1600. Taking up the office of shogun, Ieyasu made Yedo (modern Tokyo) his headquarters. Tokugawa's son, the second Tokugawa shogun, actively suppressed Christianity, while under the third shogun all Portuguese were expelled and the country was 'closed' to the outside world.

Until the mid-19th century, attempts by foreigners to 'open' Japan up for trade were firmly rejected. But in 1853 and 1854 Commodore Perry's American naval squadron forced the Yedo government to open certain ports to foreign commerce. The British, Russians, French and others all followed Perry's lead and by the 1860s foreign diplomats and traders had settled on Japanese soil. The concessions made to foreigners greatly weakened the prestige of the Tokugawa shogunate, and there was a corresponding interest in the ancient monarchy in Kyoto. In 1868 a coalition of barons from south-west Japan, acting in the emperor's name, overthrew the shogunate. The emperor, a youth still in his teens, moved his capital to Yedo, which was renamed Tokyo. He took the name Meiji (enlightened rule) as the title of his reign.

The new government began hastily to modernise Japan. The Meiji rulers also gave way to the demand for an elected national parliament. In 1889 the emperor granted a constitution, giving legislative powers to a two-chamber Diet (parliament).

Rivalry between China and Japan in Korea led to war with China in 1894, in which the Japanese were overwhelmingly successful. In 1904, a long-standing dispute with Russia over Korea boiled over into war. The fighting qualities of its conscript forces, imbued with the samurai tradition, gave Japan victory – a result which astonished the world. By the Treaty of Portsmouth, signed in 1905, Russia was forced to give up Port Arthur and cede southern Sakhalin. Japan also gained control of Korea, which was formally annexed in 1910.

Emperor Meiji's death in 1912 marked the end of a 45-year reign in which Japan had been transformed into a major world power. In the 1920s, however, there was a financial crisis, due to bank failures, followed in 1930 by the calamitous results of the great world slump. Economic disaster coincided with growing tension between Japan and China. In September 1931, without orders from Tokyo, Japanese troops attacked the Chinese, taking Mukden and other cities. The Japanese government was obliged to accept their actions. In 1933 Japan completed the occupation of all Manchuria, withdrew from the League of Nations, and recognised the so-called independent state of Manchukuo, under the last emperor of China. By 1938 Japanese forces had won control of nearly all the main cities of China.

Japan's action in China shocked international public opinion. In 1940 Japan signed a military alliance with Germany and Italy. Following a virtual trade embargo by the Allied powers, Japanese planes bombed Pearl Harbor in Hawaii, Hong Kong and Singapore in December 1941. The tide of war began to turn in June 1942, when the Japanese were defeated at sea in the Battle of Midway. Devastating air raids on Japanese cities and crippling losses at sea had brought utter defeat within sight by August 1945, when atomic bombs were dropped on Hiroshima and Nagasaki. Formal surrender took place on an American battleship in Tokyo Bay in September 1945.

Under General MacArthur, the Americans supervised far-reaching political, economic and social changes in Japan – and this process was greatly helped by the generally co-operative attitude of the Japanese government and people.

Ratification of the San Francisco peace treaty ended the occupation in April 1952. Japan's main energies were devoted not to rearmament or diplomacy, but to greater industrial production and expanding trade. Japan's increasing dominance of world trade caused concern among its competitors. Since 1956 Japan has been the world's largest shipbuilder, and in 1980 it replaced the United States as the No. 1 automaker.

In 1982 the government set about reforming the so-called 'peace constitution' by which the Japanese at the end of the Second World War renounced the right to carry arms or declare war on another country. It also attempted to improve trade relations with the United States by reducing tariffs on more than 1200 categories of products.

Japan's export success continued, however, and by 1988 the country was the world's biggest supplier of capital and donor of foreign aid. With the death of Emperor Hirohito in 1989, the longest reign in Japan's imperial history came to an end – and, with it, a symbol of continuity in a time of change.

VIETNAM AT A GLANCE
Area 127,245 square miles
Population 66,171,000
Capital Hanoi
Government Communist republic
Currency Dong = 10 hao = 100 xu
Languages Vietnamese, Chinese, French, English
Religions Buddhist (55%), Christian (8%)
Climate Tropical; temperatures vary much with seasons only in the north. Average temperature in Hanoi ranges from 17°C (63°F) in January to 29°C (84°F) in June
Main primary products Rice, cassava, sweet potatoes, bananas, maize, pineapples, coffee, tea, rubber, tobacco, pigs, cattle, timber, fish; coal, anthracite, lignite, iron, chrome, manganese, titanium, gold, phosphates, limestone, salt
Major industries Agriculture, mining, food processing, textiles, cement, cotton and silk manufacture, forestry, paper
Main exports Coal, clothing, rubber, tea, coffee
Annual income per head (US$) 150
Population growth (per thous/yr) 21
Life expectancy (yrs) Male 62 **Female** 66

Vietnam

From the early 1960s until the mid-1970s, Vietnam was torn by a violent conflict between South Vietnamese government forces, backed by the United States, and a Communist guerrilla movement, the Viet Cong, linked with armies from North Vietnam. The Communist forces were given material aid by China and the USSR. The ruthless conduct of the war and the hardship it brought to the civilian population aroused tense and often bitter controversy throughout the world.

The northern part of Vietnam was originally occupied by Indonesian peoples, with a Bronze Age civilisation. The Chinese invaded c. 100 BC, and brought northern Vietnam under control by AD 42. It was a province of the Chinese Empire until 906, and became fully independent in 938.

The Vietnamese expanded south at the end of the 15th century, conquering the kingdom of Champa, in central Vietnam. During the following century, northern Vietnam was divided by civil war and only reunited in 1592 under the rule of the Trinh family, which lasted for 200 years. But during this period the Vietnamese lost control of central Vietnam and a long war was fought between the two regions. In 1802, the whole of Vietnam was unified for the first time by the Nguyen dynasty. The French, concerned about the persecution of Catholic missionaries, invaded the south in 1859, and in 1885 established a protectorate over the rest of the country.

The opportunity for revolution against colonial rule came in the Second World War when the leading revolutionary movement, the Viet Minh, led by the Communist Ho Chi Minh, won the support of the Allies by fighting against the Japanese. With liberation in 1945, Ho proclaimed Vietnamese independence. France sent troops to reassert its control of

Vietnam in 1946. The struggle reached a climax in 1954, culminating in the defeat of besieged French forces at Dien Bien Phu. An international conference, held at Geneva in the same year, negotiated an armistice and partitioned the country.

In the early 1960s, the North Vietnamese, aiming to overthrow the South Vietnamese government, began to support a Communist uprising. By 1965 North Vietnam was involved in a full-scale war, with US troops supporting South Vietnam. Peace terms were agreed in 1973. When the US withdrew, North Vietnam occupied all of South Vietnam, setting up a Socialist regime and formally reuniting the country as the Socialist Republic of Vietnam.

After reunification in 1976, government policies led to the departure of hundreds of thousands of people, particularly those of Chinese descent. It is estimated that some 70 per cent of the refugees who left to cross the South China Sea – the so-called 'boat people' – did not survive.

Hostilities on the Cambodian and Chinese borders drew resources away from reconstruction of the economy. In December 1978 the Vietnamese invaded Cambodia, driving out the Pol Pot government and replacing it with a puppet regime supported by Vietnamese troops. China retaliated for the attack on its Cambodian ally by fighting a brief war with Vietnam in February-March 1979. Vietnam withdrew its troops from Cambodia in 1989.

Between 1980 and 1985 debate over economic reforms dominated domestic affairs. Since 1980 some economic controls have been relaxed in order to stimulate production. Peasants can freely dispose of some of their surplus produce rather than giving all of it to the state. In 1986 the reformist Nguyen Van Linh was elected leader of the Vietnamese Communist Party. His attempts to reconstruct the Vietnamese economy achieved some success, but the collapse of Communist regimes in Eastern Europe deprived the country of much of its foreign aid and investment.

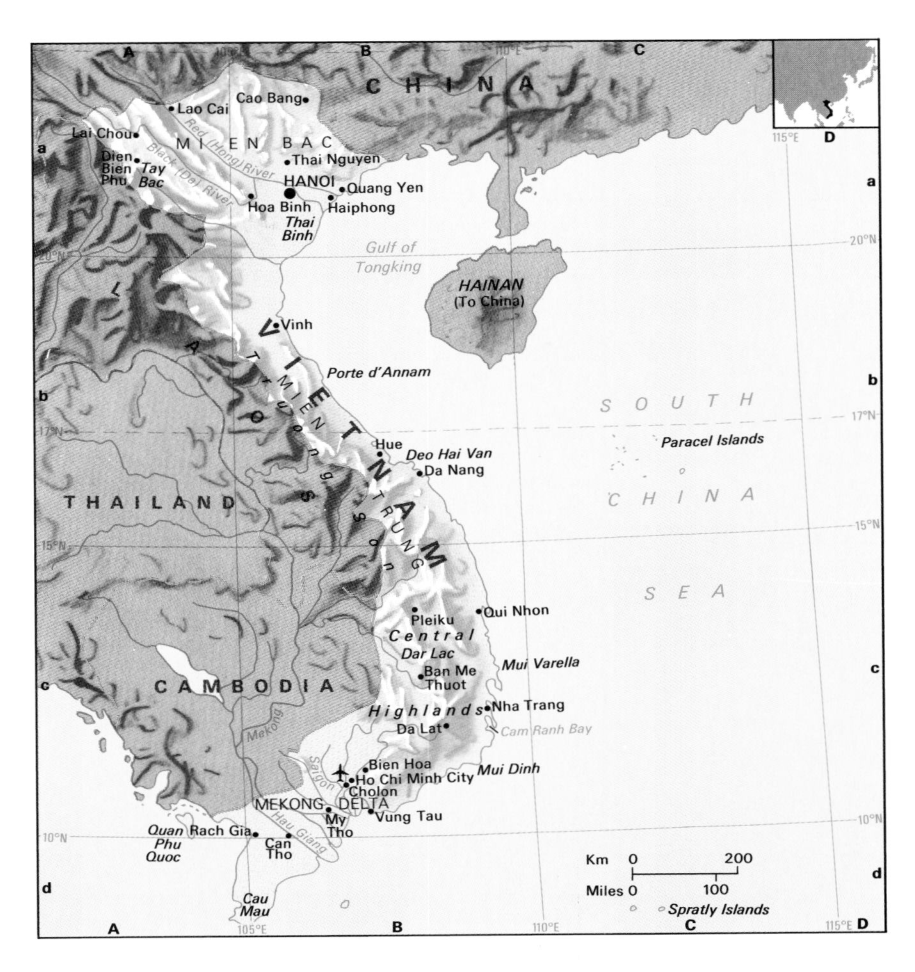

Laos

Laos was probably first settled during the 12th century by Thai tribes from south China. The earliest important Laotian state was Lan Xang, founded in 1353. In the 17th century Lan Xang enjoyed a period of peace and prosperity, and controlled parts of Vietnam and Cambodia, southern Burma and northern Thailand. But after 1694 it was split by an internal power struggle, and by 1707 three separate kingdoms had emerged, centred on Luang Prabang, Vientiane and, in the far south, Champassak.

From the end of the 18th century Laos came under the domination of the neighbouring kingdom of Thailand, but this control was challenged after 1880 by the French. In 1893, Laos became part of French Indo-China – although the Luang Prabang monarchy survived.

The Japanese occupied Laos during the Second World War, but in 1946 the French returned. In 1949, Laos was granted self-government within the French Union. In 1953, the Pathet Lao, a left-wing nationalist movement formed in North Vietnam by Prince Souphanouvong with the backing of the North Vietnamese Communists (the Viet Minh), invaded northern Laos. The civil war which followed was ended in 1954 as the result of an international conference at Geneva. In the same year, the country became fully independent.

A coalition government formed by Prince Souphanouvong and the neutralist Prince Souvanna Phouma broke down in 1959, and fighting flared up again between the Pathet Lao and government troops. A three-way struggle for power developed between Souvanna Phouma, Souphanouvong's Pathet Lao and a right-wing party under Prince Boun Oum. During this civil war, the Pathet Lao gained control of half the country. In 1962, the reconvened Geneva Conference agreed on the neutrality of Laos, and the three factions formed a coalition.

In 1963, the Pathet Lao withdrew from the government and for the rest of the decade government forces, with United States backing, fought the Pathet Lao and North Vietnamese. In 1973 the two sides reached a ceasefire agreement and in 1974 a coalition government was established. But in 1975, the Pathet Lao, again on the offensive, took the Laotian capital of Vientiane. In December 1975, the Lao People's Democratic Republic was established, with Prince Souphanouvong as the first president and Kaysone Phomvihane, the secretary-general of the Communist Party, as prime minister. After the Vietnamese invasion of Cambodia in 1978, Laotian foreign policy became increasingly aligned with that of Vietnam. At home, the government pursued a programme of 'political education'. Thousands of Laotians fled to neighbouring Thailand to escape the repression of the regime. After suffering a stroke Souphanouvong was replaced as acting president in October 1986 by Phoumi Vongvichit.

LAOS AT A GLANCE

Area 91,400 square miles
Population 4,024,000
Capital Vientiane
Government Communist republic
Currency Kip = 100 at(t)
Languages Lao, also tribal languages
Religions Buddhist (58%), tribal religions, Christian
Climate Tropical. Average temperature in Vientiane ranges from 14 to 34°C (57 to 93°F)
Main primary products Rice, maize, vegetables, tobacco, coffee, cotton; tin
Major industries Agriculture, mining and ore processing, forestry and timber milling
Main exports Timber, coffee, electricity
Annual income per head (US$) 80
Population growth (per thous/yr) 22
Life expectancy (yrs) Male 48 **Female** 51

CAMBODIA AT A GLANCE

Area 69,898 square miles
Population 6,991,000
Capital Phnom Penh
Government One-party Communist republic
Currency Riel = 100 sen
Languages Khmer (official), French
Religions Buddhist (90%), Muslim (2%), Christian (1%)
Climate Tropical; monsoon from April to October. Average annual temperature in Phnom Penh is 27°C (81°F)
Main primary products Rice, maize, bananas, rubber, livestock, tobacco, jute, timber, fish
Major industries Agriculture, fishing, forestry
Main exports Rubber, vegetables
Annual income per head (US$) 60
Population growth (per thous/yr) 22
Life expectancy (yrs) Male 47 **Female** 50

Cambodia

The people of Cambodia (formerly Kampuchea) trace their origins to a Hindu people, the Khmers, whose empire extended in medieval times from Cambodia into present-day Thailand and Vietnam. This ancient empire left magnificent temple ruins and works of sculpture, especially at its former capital of Angkor. After the 15th century, however, the power of Cambodia declined, and it lost territory to its two immediate neighbours, Thailand and Vietnam. In the 19th century it became a French protectorate. Following the Second World War, Cambodia – after achieving independence and maintaining a period of neutrality – was caught up by external conflict, becoming a battleground between Communist and non-Communist forces in the Vietnam war.

The earliest known state in Cambodia was Funan, an empire that flourished in the early centuries AD in the southern region of what is now Cambodia and in the Mekong Delta of South Vietnam. The people of Funan were skilled engineers who built a complex network of canals. Chinese travellers reported that ships could penetrate far inland on Funan's canal system. Funan derived its wealth from trade, some of which was carried on with Rome.

Funan was replaced in the 6th century by a Khmer state which the Chinese called Chenla. Hindu temples and inscriptions, identified with Chenla's culture, have been found scattered over a wide area of Cambodia.

In the 800s a Khmer king, Jayavarman II, laid the foundations of the state that later developed around the impressive city of Angkor in central Cambodia. This strong ruler founded a royal cult called devaraja, which identified the king with the Hindu god Shiva. Angkor itself became the centre of the Khmer Empire by the late 9th century and reached the height of its wealth and power under Jayavarman VII (1181 – c. 1219). His conquests extended to the Menam River (in present-day Thailand) on the west, and to Champa (now central Vietnam) on the east. But both these areas had become independent by the later 13th century, and Angkor began to decline. The Khmer Empire left behind a series of temples dating from the 9th to the 13th centuries; the finest is Angkor Wat.

During the 14th century, the Thais to the north and west began to threaten the Khmer state. Angkor itself fell to Thai forces at least twice, probably in 1369 and 1389, and by the mid-15th century the Khmer kings had abandoned it as a capital, retreating to the Mekong.

From the middle of the 17th century until the mid-19th century, the lands that were once ruled by the powerful Khmer kings began to be eaten away by Thailand and Vietnam. From 1659, Vietnamese armies, taking advantage of internal conflicts, penetrated the territory, and between 1700 and 1760 Cambodia lost the area which now forms the Mekong Delta region of South Vietnam. After 1775, the Vietnamese suffered internal disruption, but this simply gave the Thais another opportunity to interfere in Cambodia. Another partial occupation by the Vietnamese after 1834 was ended by a Cambodian revolt in 1845.

In 1861 a revolt forced King Norodom (1859-1904) to seek outside help. The French, already influential in Indo-China, imposed a French protectorate over Cambodia. Uprisings in 1865-7 and 1884-6 failed to shake French authority, which was strengthened by a new treaty in 1884.

Japan occupied much of Cambodia during the Second World War. Under Japanese pressure, Cambodia declared its 'independence' in 1944, but the following year, when Japan was defeated, the French returned. Cambodia's king, Sihanouk, negotiated a degree of self-government in 1949; full independence was granted to Cambodia at the Geneva Conference (1954) which followed France's defeat in Indo-China by the Viet Minh nationalists after eight years of fighting.

In 1955 Sihanouk nominally abdicated. He became head of state as Prince Sihanouk in 1960. His policy was one of neutrality, but after a disagreement with the United States in 1965 he leaned more towards China. In 1970 he was deposed by Prime Minister General Lon Nol. While a royal 'government-in-exile' formed around Sihanouk in Beijing, China, the monarchy was abolished and the country was renamed the Khmer Republic. Although the United States and South Vietnam supported the Lon Nol government against the insurgent Communist Khmers Rouges ('Red Khmers'), the Communists took the capital Phnom Penh, in 1975. Sihanouk was made head of state and Pol Pot the prime minister.

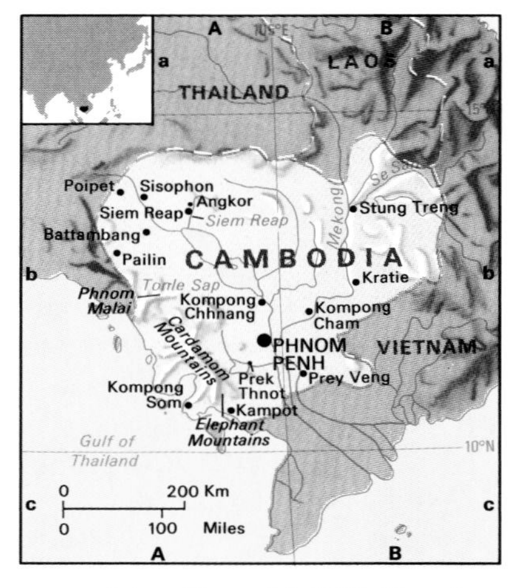

The country was renamed again, becoming Democratic Kampuchea; but it was far from democratic. Pol Pot claimed to be a political saviour who would create a unique economy based on an agricultural society and cut off from world capitalism. Towns were 'abolished' and their inhabitants, regardless of skills or age, were forced to work on the land. Personal gain was eliminated by abolishing money and property. It was an idea loosely based on Chinese leader Mao Zedong's concept for a self-reliant peasant society, but it was carried to brutal extremes. An estimated 2.5 million people were killed in what became a reign of terror during the four years of the Pol Pot regime.

Vietnam attacked the country at the end of 1978 and in January 1979 captured Phnom Penh and set up a puppet government under Heng Samrin. Pol Pot and members of the government fled to the jungles. Prince Sihanouk denounced the Vietnamese invasion, but later gave up his role as a representative of the Pol Pot government, condemning it for its atrocities.

In 1980, from his jungle headquarters, Khieu Samphan, prime minister of the Pol Pot government, announced that the Khmer Rouge had decided to reject Communism as a philosophy. In 1982 Sihanouk became president of a government-in-exile which brought together three groups opposed to the Vietnamese-backed government in Phnom Penh. Most posts in the Sihanouk government went to leaders of the former Pol Pot regime. The largest of the guerrilla groups, the Chinese-backed Khmer Rouge with an estimated 30,000 troops, was led by Pol Pot until he stepped down in 1985. The pro-Western Khmer People's National Liberation Front, with about 20,000 fighters, was led by a former prime minister, Son Sann; and Prince Sihanouk headed an army of some 5000.

An international conference in Paris in the summer of 1989 failed to solve the stalemate, although Vietnam did withdraw its troops from the country in September, precipitating renewed fighting between the guerrilla groups. In August 1990 the United Nations security council agreed to set up a Supreme National Council in Cambodia which included representatives from the government and each of the guerrilla groups. In November 1991 the Security Council agreed a plan for a ceasefire and for elections to be held under UN supervision. Prince Sihanouk returned to Cambodia at the end of 1991 and the UN peace-keeping force arrived in Cambodia in March 1992.

Thailand

Thailand (formerly Siam) was the only country of South-East Asia to avoid conquest by European powers in the 19th century. This was due in part to the stability of Thai society, strengthened by a policy of modernisation under popular monarchs.

From the 11th to the 13th centuries the first Thai migrants moved from their settlements in southern China to the area of the Menam basin. The first Thai state in the Menam lowlands was Sukhothai, established in the 13th century. By 1438, however, it had been conquered by another Thai state, with its capital at Ayutthaya. From 1549 Ayutthaya faced a succession of attacks by the Burmese until in 1568 it was overrun by Burmese forces. In 1584-7 the Thais successfully revolted against the Burmese and re-established independence. The 17th century was a golden age of peace and prosperity for Ayutthaya, but a further war with Burma from 1760 to 1767 ended with the total destruction of the city. In 1782 the present ruling Chakkri dynasty was founded, with its capital at Bangkok. Thailand expanded to conquer Chieng-Mai from the Burmese and Vientiane (Laos), as well as to dominate part of Cambodia and the northern Malay states.

From the middle of the 19th century Thailand came under pressure from the European powers, the Thais being forced to accept a series of commercial agreements; they lost Cambodia and Laos to the French and four Malay states to the British. But Anglo-French rivalry saved the rest of the country from attack, and Thailand, helped by its internal stability, managed to survive within its traditional borders.

In 1932, a group of young army officers and officials seized power and forced the monarchy to accept a constitution. The civilian leader Pridi Phanomyong was later ousted by the army. General Pibun Songkram became virtual dictator, but in 1944 he was replaced by Pridi, whose attempts to introduce parliamentary democracy failed, and in 1947 Pibun returned. Opposed to the spread of Communism, he allied Thailand with the United States. This policy was continued by succeeding military prime ministers. In 1975, Thailand demanded that the United States withdraw its planes and military personnel. The pullout in 1976 left thousands of Thais who had worked at US bases unemployed and had a serious impact on the country's economy.

A new constitution was adopted in 1977, but effective power in Thailand lay largely with the army, working with the king, Bhumibol Adulyadej. In 1980 Prem Tinsulanonda, who had been army commander, became prime minister. A steadying influence in military-civilian relations, Prem resisted pressure from the military for constitutional amendments that would have permitted military and civilian officials to hold cabinet posts. After the general election of July 1988, Prem stepped down, to be replaced by Major-General Chatichai Choonhaven.

In February 1991 a military junta deposed the prime minister. A legislative assembly was established to prepare for elections and approve a new constitution being drawn up by a constitutional commission.

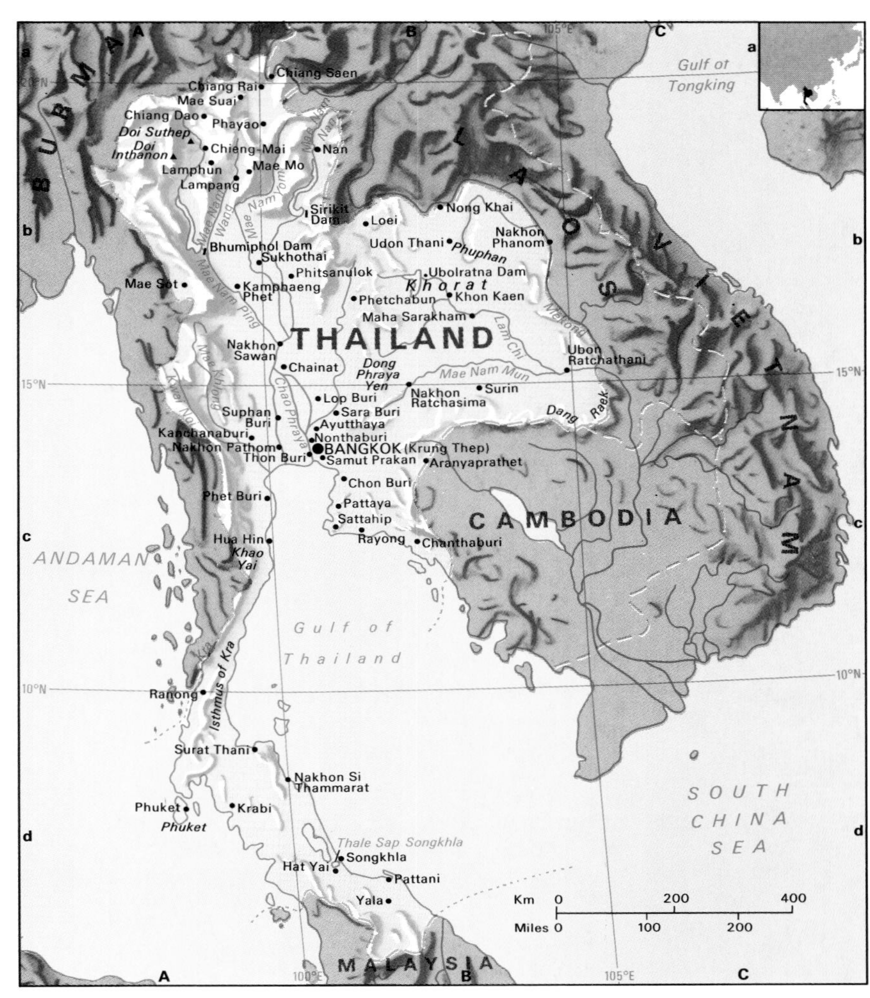

THAILAND AT A GLANCE

Area 198,720 square miles
Population 55,116,000
Capital Bangkok
Government Military-dominated monarchy
Currency Baht = 100 satang
Languages Thai
Religions Buddhist (95%), Muslim (4%)
Climate Tropical, monsoon from May to October. Temperature in Bangkok: 20°C (68°F) in December, 35°C (95°F) in April
Main primary products Rice, rubber, maize, sugar cane, cassava, pineapples, bananas, timber, fish; tin, tungsten, iron, manganese
Major industries Agriculture, processed foods, cement, paper, textiles and clothing, mining, forestry
Annual income per head (US$) 793
Population growth (per thous/yr) 13
Life expectancy (yrs) Male 64 **Female** 70

Malaysia

Almost half the world's natural rubber comes from Malaya, the dominant partner in the Federation of Malaysia. Sabah (formerly British North Borneo) and Sarawak (also on the island of Borneo), which make up the rest of Malaysia, are less developed than Malaya which has rubber plantations founded by the British in the 19th century. The growth of the rubber and tin industries brought in many Chinese immigrants; their descendants form almost 40 per cent of Malaysia's population, and their rivalry with the Malays is a source of tension.

The ancestors of the Malays arrived c. 2000 BC from Yunnan, in southern China. Two thousand years later Indian traders and monks spread throughout South-East Asia, bringing with them two new faiths, Buddhism and Hinduism. The Buddhist empire of Srivijaya, based on Sumatra, conquered much of western Malaya. It prospered on tolls from the ships using the narrow Straits of Malacca between Sumatra and Malaya. The empire lasted from the 8th to the 13th century. The 15th century saw the rise of Malacca, whose rulers became converts to Islam. Other Muslim states grew up, notably Johore, Perak and Kedah.

In 1511 Malacca fell to the Portuguese, who used it as a base for their spice trade with the Moluccas and the Far East. The Dutch wrested Malacca from them in 1641, and the Dutch in turn were ousted by the British after the Napoleonic wars. The three British bases of Singapore (founded in 1819 by Stamford Raffles on a mangrove swamp), Penang and Malacca were united in 1826 as the Straits Settlements. In 1867 the British Colonial Office took over control from the East India Company.

To begin with, the British confined their interest in Malaya to trade. Disorder in the sultanates of the interior led Britain in 1874 to establish control over Perak and Selangor, by appointing British Residents (colonial rulers). By 1914 British mastery of the peninsula was complete.

In 1841 a young British officer, James Brooke, was made rajah of Sarawak in northern Borneo after quelling a rebellion against the Sultan of Brunei. For over 100 years the 'White Rajahs', as his descendants were known, ruled Sarawak. They gained territory at the expense of Brunei, and suppressed piracy.

A London merchant, Alfred Dent, in partnership with an Austrian, Baron Overbeck, set up the British North Borneo

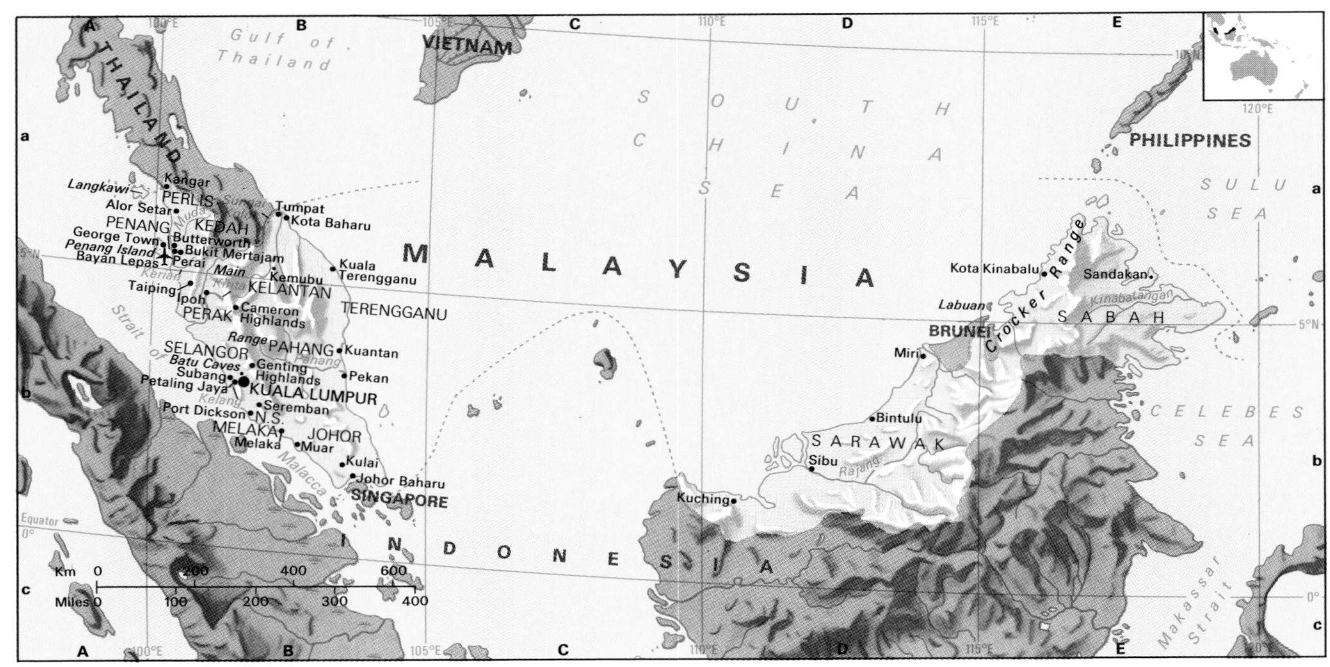

MALAYSIA AT A GLANCE
Area 127,581 square miles
Population 17,511,000
Capital Kuala Lumpur
Government Parliamentary monarchy
Currency Ringgit (Malaysian dollar) = 100 sen
Languages Malay, Chinese, English, Tamil and indigenous languages
Religions Muslim (50%), Buddhist (26%), Hindu (9%), Christian (4%)
Climate Tropical; monsoon from October to February in the east and from May to September in the west. Average daily temperature in Kuala Lumpur is 22-32°C (72-90°F)
Main primary products Rice, palm oil, rubber, timber, cocoa, pepper, pineapples, fish; crude oil, natural gas, tin, bauxite, iron ore, copper
Major industries Agriculture, crude oil production, mining, food processing, forestry, fishing, rubber, tyre manufacture, cement, electronics, chemicals, textile
Main exports Crude oil, petroleum, liquefied natural gas, timber, electronic components, palm oil, rubber, tin, pepper, cocoa, pineapples, bauxite, iron ore, copper
Annual income per head (US$) 1610
Population growth (per thous/yr) 23
Life expectancy (yrs) Male 65 **Female** 71

Company but the difficult jungle terrain forced the company into stagnation. Borneo remained economically and socially backward until 1945 when the Brooke family handed over their domain to the Colonial Office and it became a British colony.

Malaysia today is the world's leading producer of tin as well as rubber. Tin production was developed on a large scale by Chinese immigrants early in the 19th century. The rubber industry began in 1877 with 22 seedlings sent from Kew; they had been grown from seeds smuggled out of Brazil by the British explorer Henry Wickham.

Malaya and Borneo fell to the Japanese during the Second World War. Malaya's Chinese-led Communist guerrillas, seeing that Asians could defeat a Western power, turned against British troops and planters, after Japan's defeat in 1945. A state of emergency, declared in 1948, lasted until 1960, when the Communist guerrillas were defeated. A major factor in the British victory was the fortification of villages, which cut off the guerrillas from their sources of supply.

In 1948, Malaya was formed into a loose federation in which the sultanates were left with considerable powers. At that time Singapore was excluded because of Malay fears that its million Chinese would dominate the federation, and, together with the Borneo territories, it remained a Crown Colony.

The Malayan Federation became independent in 1957, and in 1963 Singapore, Sarawak and Sabah (British North Borneo) joined with it in the Federation of Malaysia; Brunei remained a British dependency until independence in 1984. Tension between the Chinese of Singapore and the Malays led to Singapore breaking away in 1965. At the same time, President Sukarno of Indonesia condemned the new country as a 'neo-colonialist' creation, and Britain had to defend the Borneo territories from Indonesian guerrilla infiltration.

Race riots between Malays and Chinese broke out in Kuala Lumpur in 1969, and the constitution was suspended. In 1970 Premier Tunku Abdul Rahman retired and was succeeded by the deputy premier, Tun Abdul Razak, who restored parliamentary rule in 1971. The government reduced some racial tension by giving more economic participation to the Malays and a greater political voice to the Chinese.

In July 1981 Datuk Seri Mahathir Mohamad became the country's fourth prime minister since independence; he was most recently re-elected in August 1986. In response to Islamic fundamentalists, particularly in peninsular Malaysia, Mahathir created an Islamic bank and an Islamic international university and initiated religious laws which made the government the final arbiter on correct Islamic observances and practices.

His attempt to amend the constitution to make royal assent to laws unnecessary ended in compromise in 1983: the sultans may not delay assent for more than thirty days. Because of long-standing Chinese-Malay tensions, the press was strictly controlled, and violators of the Internal Security Act faced the death sentence for possession of firearms or for drug trafficking.

Indonesia

The Republic of Indonesia, formerly the Dutch East Indies, was created in 1949. It consists of a vast cluster of islands stretching in a 5300 kilometre (3300 mile) arc along the equator from west of the Malay peninsula to New Guinea. It includes the islands of Java, Sumatra, Bali, the greater part of Borneo (Kalimantan), and Celebes (Sulawesi) as well as some 3000 smaller islands.

Indonesia has the fifth largest population in the world. It is inhabited by a great variety of racial groups, 300 in all, speaking 250 languages. The Muslim religion, practised by 90 per cent of the people, is a great unifying factor.

The islands of Indonesia were colonised by waves of Stone Age peoples from the mainland of South-East Asia between 2500 and 1000 BC. From AD 200 the island kingdoms derived their civilisation from India, through contacts with traders and Hindu and Buddhist monks. The 7th to 13th centuries saw the heyday of the powerful Srivijaya Empire, based on seafaring. Buddhist in culture, it was centred on southern Sumatra and controlled part of Malaya and western Java. The later Hindu empire of Majapahit ruled a large part of present-day Indonesia from 1293 to 1513.

The Islamic faith was first brought to Sumatra by Arab traders in the 13th century, and by the end of the 16th century it had displaced Hinduism and Buddhism as the dominant religion throughout Indonesia (except in the island of Bali, where Hinduism still survives). The Hindu Majapahit kingdom broke up into numerous small and weak Muslim states which were to prove no match for European penetration during the 16th century.

The East Indies had for centuries supplied Europe with spices, the Moluccas being especially noted as spice islands. The construction of new ocean-going vessels from the 15th century enabled the Europeans to trade direct with the Indies via the Cape of Good Hope, ousting the Arab traders. First on the scene were the Portuguese, who captured the vital port of Malacca on the Malay peninsula in 1511. They were followed in 1595 by the Dutch, who established themselves in western Java.

A period of intense rivalry between the Dutch and British East India companies, lasting from 1610 to 1623, ended in victory for the Dutch. The colony of Batavia (present-day Jakarta) was founded in 1619, and the Portuguese were expelled from Malacca and the Moluccas. The Dutch East India Company consolidated their hold over the islands during the 17th and 18th centuries; by 1789, when their interests were taken over by the Dutch government, they controlled much of present-day Indonesia. During the Napoleonic Wars Java fell briefly into the hands of the British and was ruled from 1811 to 1816 by Stamford Raffles, founder of Singapore. In 1824 the British and Dutch agreed on the boundaries between their spheres of influence.

The decline of the spice trade during the 18th century forced the Dutch to exploit the other natural resources of the islands, a move that brought them into conflict with the remaining semi-independent native rulers. A revolt led by Prince Diponegoro lasted for five years before being finally crushed in 1830. In the same year the notorious 'culture system' was introduced in Java by the Dutch. Peasants were required by law to devote part of their land to cash crops, such as coffee, tobacco and cotton, which were sold at a profit in Europe by Dutch firms.

The Dutch middle classes grew rich, but this period of economic exploitation left a legacy of bitterness that was to be played upon by later generations of Indonesian nationalists. Meanwhile, the Dutch completed their territorial conquests, although the Acheh sultanate in northern Sumatra was not finally subdued until 1904.

New forms of opposition arose in the 20th century, deriving in part from more sophisticated political ideas brought back from Europe by returning students. The Dutch made little or no attempt to come to terms with these stirrings of nationalism. Two Islamic nationalist groups, Budi Otomo and Sarekat Islam, were founded in the first decade of the century, but were challenged after 1919 by the newly formed Indonesian Communist Party.

Communist revolts in western Java and Sumatra in 1926 were quickly put down. From then on, until 1942, the independence movement was led by non-Communists. The Indonesian Nationalist Party was founded by Ahmed Sukarno and Mohammad Hatta in 1927. Dutch policy continued to be repressive, Sukarno spending all but two years between 1929 and 1942 in jail or in island exile, along with other nationalist leaders.

Sukarno co-operated with the Japanese during their occupation of Indonesia from 1942 to 1945, and at the end of the war proclaimed his country's independence. The returning Dutch were faced with virtual reconquest of the Dutch East Indies. In 1949 they gave up and granted the islands independence, with Sukarno as president.

Unity, political and territorial, remained a problem. Uprisings in Sumatra and Celebes against Javanese centralism in 1956-8 were suppressed with difficulty. Even more damaging was the economic decline resulting from over-ambitious foreign policy that called for large military forces, and an expensive building programme to support Sukarno's pretensions as leader of the newly independent countries of Africa and Asia. The country suffered from inflation and slump in food production; corruption was rampant.

Parliamentary democracy, introduced in 1945, was abolished by Sukarno in 1957 and replaced by an authoritarian system known as 'guided democracy'. It created a new balance of power between the politically conscious army and a revived Communist Party. During the same period, Sukarno claimed to maintain a neutralist foreign policy, though he was strongly opposed to the creation of Malaysia in 1963 – terming it Britain's 'neo-colonial creation'. In October 1965, however, the balance of forces was upset by a savage but abortive Communist coup which led to the overthrow of Sukarno and to a cruel massacre of supposed Communists in which the number killed has been variously reported as between 50,000 and 400,000.

The army, which had defeated the Communist coup, now became the dominant political force under the tight control of General Suharto. The 'confrontation' policy with Malaysia was abandoned, the Communist Party outlawed, and economic links with the West re-established. Suharto became president in 1968. Elections held in 1971 gave the army-backed government coalition a landslide victory, and Suharto was re-elected president in 1973, 1978, 1983 and 1988 – his fifth five-year term. There is opposition to President Suharto's military government. International human rights groups have claimed that the government holds thousands of political prisoners, and death squads of off-duty policemen are estimated to have killed 3000-4000 people in 1983-4.

Indonesian troops invaded and annexed the Portuguese colony of East Timor in 1975, after civil war broke out there (the western part of the island of Timor was already part of Indonesia). Since then Indonesia has poured massive economic aid into the province in an effort to develop the region quickly and eliminate support for Fretilin (Revolutionary Front for an Independent East Timor) separatists who have been engaged in sporadic guerrilla fighting with Indonesian troops since annexation. Indonesian troops are also engaged in fighting secessionist rebels in Irian Jaya, the Indonesian province that covers the western half of the island of New Guinea. In 1984-5, after an abortive uprising by OPM (Free Papua Movement) guerrillas in Jayapura, the Irian Jaya capital, an estimated 11,000 people fled to neighbouring Papua New Guinea.

INDONESIA AT A GLANCE

Area 782,660 square miles

Population 190,136,000

Capital Jakarta

Government Military-ruled republic

Currency Rupiah = 100 sen

Languages Bahasa Indonesia (official), also many other languages and dialects

Religions Muslim (88%), Christian (9%), Hindu (2%), Buddhist

Climate Tropical/monsoonal; average year-round temperature in Jakarta ranges from 23°C (73°F) to 33°C (91°F)

Main primary products Rice, maize, cassava, sweet potatoes, soya beans, sugar, bananas, palm oil, copra, rubber, coffee, tobacco, tea, groundnuts, fish, timber; oil and natural gas, tin, nickel, copper, bauxite, coal

Major industries Agriculture, oil and gas production and refining, mining, forestry, fishing, textiles, transport equipment assembly, food processing, paper, cement, matches, tyres, glass, chemicals, fertilisers

Main exports Crude oil, natural gas, refined petroleum products, timber, rubber, tin and other metal ores, coffee, fish products, tea, tobacco

Annual income per head (US$) 520

Population growth (per thous/yr) 18

Life expectancy (yrs) Male 58 **Female** 63

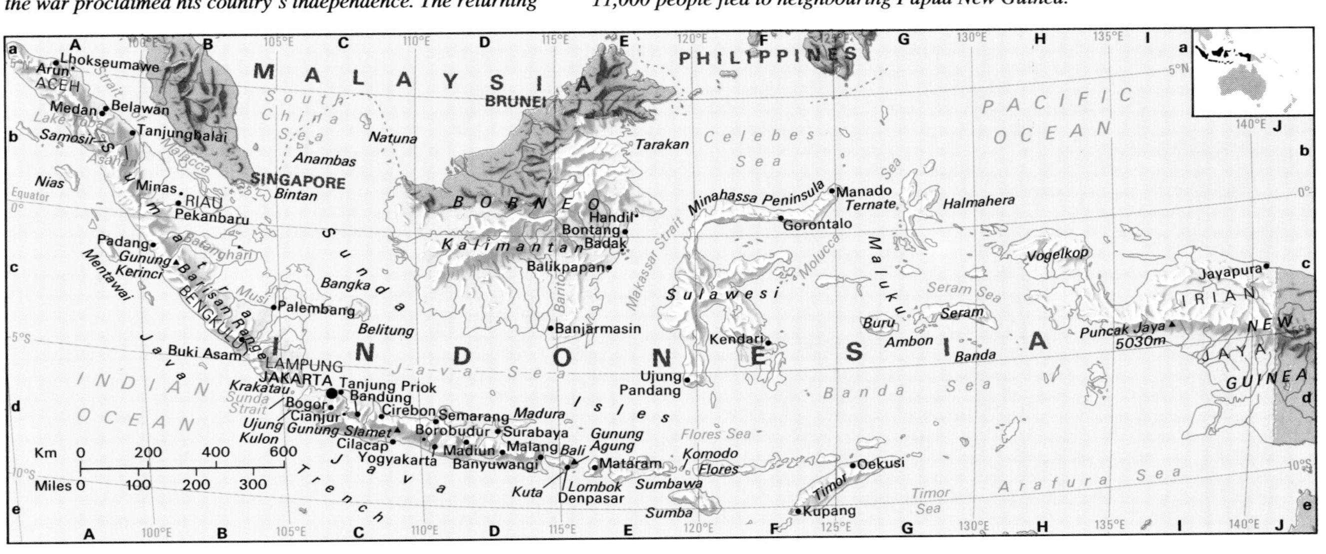

Picture Credits

p.9 Marthelot-Scope; p.10 Buisson-Vandystadt; p.11 Abrial-Pix; p.12 left Abrial-Pix; right Silvester-Rapho; p.13 Gerster-Rapho; p.14 left Hopker-Magnum; right Buisson-Vandystadt; p.15 Marthelot-Scope; p.16 Dupuis-Fotogram; p.17 top Huguier-Explorer; bottom Marthelot-Scope; p.18 top Marthelot-Scope; bottom Macintyre-A.Hutchison Lby; p.19 left Abrial-Pix; right Perno-Explorer; p.20 left Brake-Rapho; right Silvester-Rapho; p.21 top Yamashita-Rapho; bottom left Éts Bisson, Paris; bottom right S. Held; p.22 top left Yamishita-Rapho; top right Macintyre-A.Hutchison Lby; bottom Yamashita-Rapho; p.23 Macintyre-A.Hutchison Lby; p.24 Rapho; p.25 top C.Lénars; bottom C.Lénars; p.26 left Marthelot-Scope; right Berry-Magnum; p. 27 Buisson Vandystadt; p.28 Perno-Explorer; p.29 S.Held; p.30 Macintyre-A.Hutchison Lby; p. 31 left C.Lénars; right C.Lénars; p.32 Marthelot-Scope; p.33 left Baumgartner-Explorer; right Mayer-Magnum; p.34 Burri Magnum; p.34/5 Schwab-Fotogram; p.35 Abrial-Pix; p.36 Hopker-Magnum; p.37 Abrial-Pix; p.38 Marthelot-Scope p.39 top Charlier-Ana; bottom Buisson-Vandystadt; p.40 Buruma-Ana; p.41 top Macintyre-A.Hutchison Lby; bottom Charlier-Ana; p.42 top Huguier-Explorer; bottom Buisson-Vandystadt; p.43 left Marthelot-Scope; right Huguier-Explorer; p.44 left Hopker-Magnum; right Macintyre-A.Hutchison Lby; p.45 top Hopker-Magnum; bottom Macintyre-A.Hutchison Lby; p.46 Marthelot-Scope; p.46/7 Launois/Rapho; p.47 Macintyre-A.Hutchison Lby; p.48 Marthelot-Scope; p.49 Griffiths-Magnum; p.50 Griffiths-Magnum; p.51 F.Roche; p.52 Labbe-Gamma; p.52/3 F.Roche; p.53 Rossi-Image Bank; p.54 Labbe-Gamma; p.55 Moineau-Explorer; p.56 top Fournie-Explorer; bottom Labbe-Gamma; p.57 top Fournie-Explorer; bottom Fournie-Explorer; p.58 Abbas-Gamma; p.59 Perno-Explorer; p.60 Blum-Diaf; p.61 Raynaud-Vloo; p.62 Gamma; p.63 top Blum-Diaf; bottom Blum-Diaf; p.64 Tikhomiroff-Magnum; p.65 Blum-Diaf; p.66 top Griffiths-Magnum; bottom Griffiths-Magnum; p.67 Griffiths-Magnum; p.68 Griffiths-Magnum; p.69 Yamashita-Rapho; p.70 Gabanou-Diaf; p.71 top Michaud-Rapho; bottom S.Held; p.72 Mayer-Magnum; p.73 Tomkins-A.Hutchison Lby; p.74 S.Held; p.75 top C.Lénars; bottom Deshayes-Rapho; p.76 left Gabanou-Diaf; right Roques-Top; p.77 S.Held; p.78 Mayer-Magnum; p.79 left Souricat-Explorer; right Dumas-Fotogram; p.80 top left Menis-Diaf; top right Moisnard-Explorer; bottom Huguier-Explorer; p.81 Yamashita-Rapho; p.82 S.Held; p.83 top Canoen-Diaf; bottom Marthelot-Scope; p.84 left L.Boucaud; right Wheeler-Rapho; p.85 left S.Held; right Dumas-Fotogram; p.86 Montbazet-Explorer; p.87 top Launois-Rapho; bottom Dumas-Fotogram; p.88 Macintyre-A.Hutchison Lby; p.89 Huguier-Explorer; p.90 S.Held; p.90/91 M.Dominik; p.92 C.Lénars; p.93 left J.Bottin; right Top; p.94 Boutin-Explorer; p.95 top Dichter Lourié-Pix; bottom Dumas-Fotogram; p.96 Dumas-Fotogram; p.97 top Dichter Lourié-Pix; bottom Dichter Lourié-Pix p.98 S.Held; p.99 C.Lénars; p.100 left C.Lénars; right C. Lénars; p.101 C.Lénars; p.102 Boutin-Explorer; p.103 S.Held; p.104 Dichter Lourié-Pix; p.105 left Valentin-Explorer; right J.M.Steinlein; p.106 top Dupuy-Pix; bottom Lamontagne-Diaf; p.107 Olivry-Pix; p.108 Berenger-Pix; p.109 Mayer-Magnum; p.110 top Fields-Rapho; bottom Fusco-Magnum; p.111 Koch-Rapho; p.112 J.Bottin; p.113 C.Lénars; p.114 Bellone-Fotogram; p.114/5 Jaffre-Durou; p.115 J.Bottin; p.116 top left C.Lénars; top right C.Lénars; bottom C.Lénars; p.117 Barbey-Magnum; p.118 P.Frilet; p.119 left C.Lénars; right Gerster-Rapho; p.120 C.Lénars; p.121 C.Lénars; p.122 C.Lénars; p.123 top Langiaux-Fotogram; bottom C.Lénars; p.124 C.Lénars; p.125 Grismayer-Pix; p.126 Lolliot-Fotogram; p.127 Delcourt-Rapho; p.128 Latude-Gamma; p.129 left C.Lénars; right Latude-Gamma; p.130 S.Held; p.131 Latude-Gamma; p.132 left Gray-Gamma; right Barbey-Magnum; p.133 Ayer-Rapho; p.134 top Macintyre-Gamma; bottom J.Bottin; p.135 C.Lénars; p.136 S.Held; p.137 top Couteau-Top; bottom S.Held; p.138 Barbey-Magnum; p.139 Latude-Gamma; p.140 Pix; p.141 C.Lénars; p.142 Pix; p.143 J.Bottin; p.144 left D.Jeu; right C.Lénars; p.145 top Lolliot-Fotogram; bottom C.Lénars; p.147 top Muller-Cedri; bottom Gohier-Explorer; p.148 Muller-Cedri; p.149 Muller-Cedri; p.150 Muller-Cedri; p.151 top Muller-Cedri; bottom Gohier-Explorer; p.152 Gohier-Explorer.

Cover pictures
Top: Elliott Erwitt-Magnum
Bottom: Marc Riboud-Magnum

74-006-1